VISNOSTIC™ SELLING

The Power of
VISualization DiagNOSTIC Statements
A Neuroscientific approach to
client centric sales, marketing, and leadership.

Kimberlee Slavik

Illustrated by David A. Wiener
Foreword by Michael T. Bosworth

DEDICATION

Dedicated to all of my wonderful clients for helping me understand how to make sales an honorable, respected, strategic, intelligent, and rewarding process.

SPECIAL THANKS

Thank you to David Wiener. He has been my mentor and business partner since 2002. He is a great leader with an incredible business mind. Collaborating feels natural but I had no idea he is also extremely artistic. His artwork is a critical component of this content.

To my friends brave enough to be my guinea pigs as I was writing, your feedback has made this book what it is today. Thank you!

Thank you to those that embraced my coaching and leadership through the years, and thank you to those that didn't; both proved the points in this book.

And finally, thank you to Scott Slavik, my husband for over 30 years. You amaze me for always supporting and believing in my unconventional approach to pretty much everything.

VISNOSTIC™ SELLING
The Power of
Visualization Diagnostic Statements
A Neuroscientific approach to
client centric sales, marketing, and leadership.
Author: Kimberlee Slavik

Copyright © 2019 by Kimberlee Slavik www.dynaexec.com
Illustrations by David A. Wiener

ISBN: 978-1-7321916-1-7
Library of Congress Cataloging-in-Publication is available
Design & Layout by: Douglas DoNascimento
Published by: Briggs & Schuster
BSA.IM

Printed in the United States of America

VISualization DiagNOSTIC Statements™

Defined

VISualization

verb (used without object)
to recall or form mental images or pictures.

DiagNOSTIC

adjective
of, relating to, or used in diagnosis.
serving to identify or characterize; being a precise indication.

Statement

noun
something stated.
a communication or declaration in speech or writing, setting forth facts, particulars, etc.

CONTENTS

FOREWORD

By

Michael T. Bosworth,

Best Selling Author

Of

  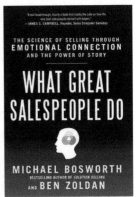

When Kimberlee asked me to read this book, I began skimming, as I always do, until I came to the worksheet with a list of what Kim calls Visualization Diagnostic Statements. I have been talking about a buyer's 'vision of a solution' since 1979. My problem over the years has been the resistance of most senior marketing executives to convert from "Product Marketing" to "Customer Usage Marketing."

I stopped reading this book after chapter one because I couldn't help thinking about how I was going to use it in my sales training business. Chapter one gave ME a vision of how I could finally defeat the problem of companies leading with product features, presentations and demos – a problem I have been wrestling with for 40 years! I sent Kimberlee 23 Visualization Diagnostic Statements that I was able to create in less than 10 minutes. I then went back and read the book from front to back. For you to understand why I got so excited, I should tell you some of my story.

I will be eternally grateful for my opportunity to join the cloud computing division of Xerox called Xerox Computer Services (XCS) in 1972. The ten years I spent there shaped my concepts of buying and selling "high difficulty" products and services. High difficulty meaning the majority of potential buyers in target markets don't know why they need it or how they would use it. High difficulty products, services and technology that are conceptual, intangible, perceived as expensive, sold to committees. High difficulty offerings that are so new to the market that there is no budget line item for what they sell.

❝ When Kimberlee Slavik asked me to read this book, I began skimming as I always do until I came to the worksheet with a list of what Kim calls Visualization Diagnostic Statements.

At XCS, we were selling first-generation cloud computing. Founded in 1969, Xerox Computer Services had 50 Los Angeles based customers when I joined them in 1972. XCS customers communicated their real-time business transactions over dumb terminals – transactions like journal entries, time cards, sales orders, production orders, etc. In case you think Software-as-a-Service is a new thing, our customers paid us three ways for the usage of our applications. We charged them for the amount of storage their data took up on our very expensive, at the time, disk drives. We billed our customers for reports by the print line, and we charged them for every business transaction. Each "enter" was 2.2 cents. Our business revenue model was based on customer usage. No *usage*, no *revenue*. All XCS employees, in all silos, were focused on keeping those 50 customers online and processing their business transactions. Local government offices, distribution companies and manufacturing companies did their daily functional jobs on our system.

After my initial 6 weeks of what we called "product school" (It was actually training on how to demo our applications) I started on the help desk. Over the next year, I learned how different job titles in different departments used our business applications to run their businesses using our "cloud-based" Interactive Accounting System. For my second year with XCS, I was field support for virtually every job title that touched our system. After two years of helping customers, I reluctantly took a 'promotion' to territory salesperson in 1974. I was 28 years old at the time. The majority of my fellow sellers were former IBM salespeople in their mid to late 30s. I had observed over my first two years with the company that typically, they would make their first sale 9 to 15 months after their hire date. In 1974, in my first five months on quota, I sold more than any other salesperson had sold in the history of our company in a full year.

I will share with you my 20/20 hindsight on why I was able to do that. It was completely intuitive at the time. My two years supporting our customers enabled me to sell customer usage, job title by job title. I had a 60-second story for job titles I would cold call. The Controller and the Materials Manager were my favorite entry points into new potential customers. Each story was about a specific job title, the way he/she used to do it, and a vision of a solution statement at the top of the story arc – "He told me he wished he could update his production plan overnight if one of his suppliers were going to be late." I would finish the stories with a business result – "he decided to take the risk of becoming our first MRP client 18 months ago. Inventory levels have dropped from x to y, etc." The majority reacted very positively to the peer stories I shared with them. [Most people are curious about their peers.] I would then ask, "What's going on around here?" I knew the story worked when they would invite me to take a tour of their business. I would then start offering up "What if you had the ability to?" questions based on my first-hand knowledge of how his peer was using my system.

❝❝ I have been talking about a buyer's 'vision of a solution' since 1979. My problem over the years has been the resistance of most senior marketing executives to convert from "Product Marketing" to "Customer Usage Marketing."

Once they had a vision of a solution, I still had to prove our offering would fulfill their vision statements. Prove how our applications would allow them to do their jobs better than they were currently doing them. That is when I would bring in a product expert for a demo. Not before. My demos were 45 minutes. My fellow sellers' demos were 8 hours long. Why? Because we all went through a six-week "demo school" right after we were hired. We hired them in batches so we could train them all at once. Each product manager had stage time. We couldn't 'graduate' until we could demo every application. At the end of demo school, all my classmates went into sales and luckily for me, because I was right out of college and didn't know anything, I went to work on the help desk. When they went on sales calls, the ONLY thing we had trained them on was how to give a demo. So, they would offer up a demo within the first 60 seconds of every new prospect call they made. The reason it took them 9 – 15 months to make their first sale was that's how long it took them to TRANSLATE the product feature knowledge they got in demo school into the solution expertise they would need to propose specific visions of solutions to specific job titles. I had the luxury of helping XCS clients USE our applications for two years before I went into sales. Unfortunately, even today, most technology companies force their new sellers, new clients and customers to do that translation from the product features on massive presentation decks to HOW they would USE specific features SITUATIONALLY to do their jobs better. I call this translation period "Time-to-solution expertise."

When I became a rookie Branch Manager for XCS in 1979, I knew I had to figure out a way to dramatically reduce the 9 – 15-month time-to-solution expertise for the new salespeople I was hiring. My solution? The birth of the critical components of Solution Selling – the 9-Box "behaviorally correct" questioning matrix combined with the "Pain Sheet." Pain Sheets were discovery questions for each targeted buyer, written by the person in our organization who had the most knowledge of how a particular job function (i.e., Controller or Materials Manager) USED our applications to plan, strategize, process, make money, save money, achieve goals, solve problems. The left side had the intelligent diagnostic questions, and the right side had the "vision of a solution" questions, potential usage questions – "When X happens, what if you were able to...?" I wrote these sales tools myself for the salespeople in my branch. I had them practice with me before they used them on sales calls. All these customer usage questions were easily proven when it came time for a demo. In my branch, I allowed no demos until the seller documented a particular buyer's vision of a solution. The role of our product became PROOF of vision, rather than education, training, interest arousal, etc. About that time, XCS realized they needed to support our sellers with a deeper knowledge of both our user buyers and financial buyers in specific market segments. We called this new Department "Industry Marketing." Sellers had three Industry Marketing experts available to help them sell. (One for Distribution, one for Manufacturing and one for Public Service clients.) At the end of 1979 where my Philadelphia branch was "Branch of the Year," XCS moved me back to our LA Headquarters to work on the time-to-solution expertise problem for the entire organization.

The most significant insight in my last years at XCS came from working with Neil Rackham on the SPIN project in 1979. Besides the 80/20 problem (20% of the sellers bring in 80% of the revenue) another more sinister problem bobbed up to the surface. Rackham discovered that each new 'batch' of newly hired Xerox copier sellers would steadily get better every month for their first 18 months, and then, "*you can set your watch by it*," they would fall into a slump. The irony is at the height of their hard-earned solution expertise, they became impatient. Now, because they finally had gained solution expertise, they would hear four words out of a buyer's mouth about his or her problem, and they would jump in with the "here's what you need" to solve it. The irony was, they were correct, they DID understand the need and the precise Xerox "solution" to that need, but they pushed so hard, the buyers pulled away. Most of us do not like other people telling us "you need to." This behavior also demonstrated a lack of empathy. They expected a buyer to come to the same vision of a solution in four seconds that it took them 18 months to understand. [I should have paid more attention – more on this later.]

When I started my Solution Selling business in 1983, my mission was to help my VP of Sales clients to "lift" their bottom 80% sellers. To do that, I knew I had to convert my clients from product feature marketing and training to customer usage marketing and training.

To make this point, let me share a quick story. 20+ years ago I was teaching a public Solution Selling workshop in Del Mar, California. At the start of the workshop I went around the room, asking each participant what they sell.

Most attendees were selling some kind of technology based, B2B productivity improving hardware/software/consulting to a committee of risk averse buyers. I got around to 'Richard,' and I asked him what he sells. He responded, "Mike, I sell glue." I then said, "Tell me about the glue." He was a chemical engineer selling industrial adhesives and got into a very detailed description of the 'glue' – bonding strength, resistance to heat fluctuations, mold and vibration, etc. I watched the eyes of the rest of the participants roll up into their heads. I stopped him and said, "Richard, it sounds to me like you are using the word glue as a NOUN. Can you change it to a VERB and tell me about your product?" He was a smart guy (Masters in CE from MIT). He immediately switched to the customer's USAGE of his glue. Now everybody in the room understood how Richard's clients used his industrial adhesives without having to have a degree in chemical engineering.

> **❝❞ Chapter one gave ME a vision of how I could finally defeat the problem of companies leading with product features, presentations and demos – a problem I have been wrestling with for 40 years!**

From 1983 through today, client after client, I encountered extreme resistance to my customer usage ideas by people in product marketing. There are many surface reasons why I meet resistance. For many of them, their vast, in-depth knowledge of technology and their products is their source of power in their organization. They are product experts. Once people taste power, they want to keep and expand it. It took me years to finally understand another deep, subtle and shameful underlying reason so many Product Marketing people (90% of my experience is selling technology to the enterprise) resisted my customer usage ideas. Many product experts had no hands on experience with customers using their products! They were product experts, not customer experts. They *didn't know* how their customers USED their offerings to make money, save money, achieve goals, solve problems or satisfy their needs. They thought of their product as a noun instead of a verb.

Over the years, I was able to find some innovators and early adopters who saw something in Solution Selling that it took me years to understand and articulate; they saw Solution Selling as the world's greatest *product usage training*. I thought I was doing sales training.

What they really hired me to do was to teach their sellers to diagnose and prescribe customer usage solutions to the problems of their clients. Had I been smart enough to position Solution Selling as product usage training for difficult-to-sell products and services, I believe I would have ten times as much money in the bank as I do today.

I had no idea how difficult it would be to get 'product experts' to create the discovery question tools we needed to train their salespeople. We needed customer stories and customer usage statements for each defined 'buyer persona' they wanted their salespeople and channel partners to sell to. It never occurred to me that they didn't really understand how their clients and customers used their offerings.

I also had another underlying problem that took me twenty years to finally figure out. My primary champion/sponsor/power buyer was the VP of Sales. Here was the symptom – my VP of Sales client would say to me, *"Mike, I just don't understand it. The top 20% of my sellers LOVE Solution Selling. They are all selling even more. But, the bottom 80% quit using it within two weeks of the workshop!"* I founded Solution Selling to help the VP of Sales 'lift' his/her bottom 80%. It wasn't helping them lift their bottom 80% like it was supposed to! The symptom did not lead me to figure out the reason and the solution until 2008.

❝❞ I sent Kimberlee 23 Visualization Diagnostic Statements that I was able to create in less than 10 minutes.

In 2008, I got my wakeup call. I found out that Sales Benchmark Index (SBI) had completed a recent study of 1100 B2B sales organizations. The 80/20 problem was now worse than it had ever been. 13% of the sellers in that study brought in 87% of the revenue. This motivated me to finally diagnose the "bottom 80% quit using it" problem. As it turns out, when top 20% sellers engage with new prospects, they intuitively know that they have to build some connection and trust before they bring out their discovery question tools. The bottoms 80%, because they don't connect intuitively, go to their tools too soon. The buyer pulls back emotionally and physically. They are thinking, "you don't know me well enough to ask me these types of questions." That's why the bottom 80% quit using the tools – their potential buyers were pushing them away. Most of us will let non-sales professions ask us pretty deep questions in our first-time meetings with them – lawyers, doctors, financial planners can all begin asking profound diagnostic questions almost immediately. Salespeople can't. There is too much history. Too many of us have visceral memories of feeling taken advantage of, pushed or pressured into doing something we soon regretted, by salespeople.

❝ I stopped reading this book after chapter one because I couldn't help myself thinking about how I was going to use it in my sales training business.

Thus, this was the birth of *What Great Salespeople Do*. When I was a rookie sales trainer at Xerox, I got trained in Xerox's flagship sales training methodology, Professional Selling Skills (PSS). In that training, they overtly told us that we can educate sellers to be more competent, but we cannot teach them how to connect. They told me that rapport and connection were "chemistry," and the chemistry between every two human beings is unique. In 2008, I learned there was actual neuroscience supporting how humans react to both the anticipation of a story as well as the stories themselves. This motivated me to learn how to use the power of story – building stories, telling stories and tending buyer stories – to help the bottom 80% of humanity in *all* professions, not just sales, to establish an emotional connection and trust with strangers quickly. In this book there is also neuroscience explaining the profound yet simple 'reframe' from questions to statements, for diagnosing instead of qualifying and of course, the power of visualization!

At Mike Bosworth Leadership, we use a story framework to help sellers build trust and connection *before* they get out their sales process, their presentation decks (yuck), their qualification questions, their feature presentation – whatever selling system their senior sales management is forcing them to use.

To get a VP of Sales to buy into something 'soft' like story building, telling and tending, he/she really has to be motivated to change. As it turns out most sales VPs also have deep shame about a problem they don't like talking about. Most VPs of Sales are former top 20% sellers who sold intuitively. They do not know how to coach their bottom 80% sellers to do what they did intuitively – connect and build trust. Now they have a way.

I have been fighting the product marketing problem since 1983. For a while, I thought I was gaining some traction. Once presentation software came along, I knew I was fighting a losing battle.

❝ Kim's methodology makes it as easy to buy complex technology, as it is to buy a consumer product.

My latest anti-Product Marketing campaign involves helping sellers eliminate ONE three-word phrase that is lengthening time-to-solution expertise for sellers and clients as well as *ruining* potential customer buying cycles. That phrase is *"our solution will…"*

This problem, as Kimberlee points out so well in this book, is the way most B2B technology companies are teaching their new salespeople AND their new customers to think about their product – as an "it" – giving it a life of its own – "IT will do this an IT will do that." [How will IT do it? Do we plug IT in or does it have a battery?]

This book will allow organizations to finally understand the difference between leading with product features and leading with a tempting list of peer user capability statements. This book will enable your organization to live up to the subtitle on my 1993 book, Solution Selling – *Creating Buyers in Difficult Selling Markets*. Kim's methodology makes it as easy to buy complex technology, as it is to buy a consumer product.

I recommend organizations selling high difficulty offerings appoint a Director of Customer Usage Marketing. The initial mission of the Customer Usage Marketing Department is to HARVEST the stories of your most successful clients and customers. You will want stories of how your best clients and customers are *using* your stuff to do their jobs better in order to achieve competitive advantages. In addition to selling more, your clients will be able to take better care of THEIR customers. Each story will yield (in the *"she told us she needed a way to"* section of the story) a customer usage statement that can be used to build your Visualization Diagnostic Statement worksheets.

This book teaches sales & marketing how to entice specific targeted buyers with specific solution visualization statements (Statements, not questions.). Statements allow the buyer to 'opt-in' or not. In either case, you will be happy to discover that statements don't trigger the typical avoidance responses most sellers elicit.

❝❞ In this book there is also neuroscience explaining the profound yet simple 'reframe' from questions to statements, for diagnosing instead of qualifying and of course, the power of visualization!

With Visualization Diagnostic Statements, sellers can nurture their potential client's buying cycle with a list of tantalizing capabilities where the only decision the buyer has to make is either "I wish I could say this," or "I can say this today." If these customer usage statements are targeted and tantalizing, your prospects will react to them. Once your buyers checks "I would like to say this," that statement becomes an *affirmation*. My wife is a therapist and has written articles on the power of affirmations. Affirmations are powerful. They show us what we want. Can you think of a better motivation to buy for your prospects to WANT something that your offering can provide them? (BEFORE you show it to them!)

Once your prospect makes her affirmations, THEN as the seller, you can demonstrate command of your company resources by getting your product experts to prove your product can deliver on the affirmation or what I call a buying vision. [Now you get to demo (finally!) but only the features that deliver on the vision. You will have much shorter demos.]

❝❞ **This book shows how recent neuroscience demonstrates the power of visualization and affirmation.**

For each Customer Usage Statement, there should be a 60-second "Customer Hero Story" backing it up. These stories create multiple emotional buying reasons – peer curiosity to agree to listen to a peer story, and if the story hits home, peer envy. Peer envy is a compelling reason to try something new. They also lead buyers to the emotional conclusions that this seller is authentic; this seller understands the difficulty of my situation and hope that this seller might be able to help me. Customer hero stories also help millennial sellers overcome age and gender disparities establishing trust and credibility. People make emotional decisions for logical reasons. Product proof of vision sessions gives them the logical reasons to justify their emotional buying decisions.

The initial mission of your new Customer Usage Marketing department is to 'harvest' the customer usage stories from your best clients and customers. These stories will produce customer usage statements. These customer usage statements can be used on what I will call for now "Potential Solution Worksheets for Targeted Buyers." These worksheets enable your salespeople and channel partners to intelligently position your capabilities as potential solutions for targeted buyers during sales conversations. As Neil Rackham told me in 1979, *"the best sales calls are conversations, not presentations."*

This book shows how recent neuroscience demonstrates the power of visualization and affirmation. Great leaders create a vision and lead people to it. Great salespeople help their buyers develop a vision of a solution, affirm they want it and then help them buy it by proving it with their technology and resources. We can train new salespeople in a matter of weeks to offer a targeted buyer a 60-second peer story, with a hero, a story arc, a struggle and of course, a vision of a solution – "She told me she needed a way to..." At the end of the story, the seller can transition and see if the story worked: "Enough about me, what's going on around here?" If the buyer is warm, and trusting, the seller can offer some 'solution ideas' collected from other peer clients. I see them moving to the same side of the desk as the buyer (or sharing their screen if selling remotely) and saying, "let's go through the capabilities other CFOs are using from our offering and see if you relate to any of them." For each peer usage statement, three simple choices: (1) I would like to say this, or (2) I can say this today, or (3) This one does not apply to me. [So far, with this new prospect, no presentation, no bullet points, no product features!] Once the buyer selects the customer usage statements he/she relates to, they become affirmations. Now your sellers can employ your product experts to assist in proving your offering will deliver the affirmed capabilities. Each statement should be mapped to specific best ways to prove the product can deliver on the vision.

Your Customer Usage Marketing Department can train new sellers on how your clients, customers and targeted buyers are able to use your offerings to make money, save money, achieve goals and solve problems. Teach them to use potential solution worksheets before they start making sales calls. Existing Product Marketing departments can transition to be becoming the Product Proof of Capabilities depament.

❝❝ Most humans love to buy and hate to feel sold to. Using Visualization Diagnostic Statements will help your clients and customers enthusiastically buy from you.

As you take this book to heart, try developing a few of these Visnostic Statements for yourself.

A Buyer may WISH to say "My vendors truly understand my business and effectively explain how they can help me." A Marketing Executive may WISH to say "Our message is no longer based upon features and functions and instead focus on client results." A Sales Executive may WISH to say "My clients are happy that they no longer have to translate features and functions into ways in which they will benefit from my offering." And a Sales Leader may WISH to say things such as "We have dramatically reduced time-to-solution expertise for both my new salespeople and our new clients and customers." "Our sales cycles are shorter and faster." "A higher percentage of my sellers and channel partners achieve their quotas." "I use my finite, expensive technical resources only on opportunities where my sellers developed buying visions first." "Our win percentage has increased dramatically."

Most humans love to buy and hate to feel sold to. Using Visualization Diagnostic Statements will help your clients and customers enthusiastically buy from you.

EARLY REACTIONS*
TO
VISNOSTIC SELLING
AND
TRANSLATION WORKSHOPS

Comments are from a diverse group of talent and experience including a Teacher, Politician, Visualization Expert, Direct Sales, Solution Architect, Channel Sales, Marketing, Ad Agency, Authors and Buyers. This book is written for everybody.

Quotes after reading the draft of this book and conducting the first workshop in October, 2018

Matthew Dixon, best selling coauthor of The Challenger Sale, The Challenger Customer and The Effortless Experience

"This is a a great read--thought-provoking, engaging and super practical. It really gets to the heart of what great salespeople do naturally, but many average performers and newer reps struggle with: the ability to create a conversation that leads TO their solution, rather than WITH their solution. I'd highly recommend Kimberlee Slavik's terrific book to anybody looking to take their selling approach to the next level."

Jennifer, Sales Channel Marketing & Sales Executive for a Fortune 500 Company (Top 60 with $28 Billion in annual revenue)

"With Kim's help we have been able to shift our focus from educating the customer about a specific product to

identifying gaps in a customers desired end state and focus our attention on their needs versus our speeds & feeds. The Visnostic Statement method is a powerful tool to get your customers excited about the benefits without ever mentioning the products and services. It's ingenious – easy for sellers as they are simply getting to know their customer better and easy for customers because we are not asking them to make the connections between our offerings and their environment."

"As I read 'Visnostic Selling' a light bulb went off in my head; we had been doing it all wrong. No wonder the message wasn't resonating with customers, we were starting with meeting 3. By working with Kim to translate our "Meeting 3" marketing presentation into Visnostics Statements suitable for a first meeting with the customer, we are able to "diagnose" the customer and cater subsequent presentations to their specific needs (that we learn through the visnostic statement scoring). It's brilliant! We've turned a first meeting monologue into an engaging dialogue. Sellers love it. Customers love it. We are making it EASY and engaging for everyone. Thank you Kim! "

David Wiener, Senior Sales Leader

"During my selling career of 50 years, I read all the sales books and even taught some. I believe the perceived needs of the customer and the apparent solutions to these needs have always controlled the relationship between seller and buyer. This, the weakest point in the sales cycle has never been fully addressed until now.

For the last ten years, Kim Slavik has worked on a method for establishing the real customer needs and their priorities. She has also created an easily understood way of establishing and presenting these needs and priorities.

Visualization Diagnostic Statements will change the way selling is performed. It is a win-win for buyer and seller. I am honored to have worked with Kim and illustrated her book."

Sherry Hall, Award Winning Author and Educator

"While Kim's work most certainly has the potential to be life-changing for salespeople, it also holds implications beyond the world of business. As an educator, I have seen first hand the power of visualization. I believe Kim's groundbreaking book can create positive change across multiple settings."

Phil White former Sales VP, Computer Associates

"A refreshing common sense approach of engaging customers and prospects from their perspective. A must read for any modern day sales organization."

James "Jim" Hester, Solution Architect, Pre and Post Sales Support

"As a pre-sales solution architect with decades of industry experience, I've noticed certain characteristics that make sales teams more successful than others. A successful sales team must listen more than they speak and absorb everything they see and hear. Although you might think I'm spelling out "Solution Selling," after reading Kim's innovative book you will find that products coupled together do not yield a solution and customers know it. Customers want to differentiate their products and services to their customers but before they can their vendors and partners must listen,

prioritize, and gain acceptance of future directions. It is too often assumed that we (as salespeople) truly understand the customer's business almost without any interaction; after all we have a solution for everything. Building and interpreting Visnostic Statements will accelerate a longer, more valued relationship with your customers putting you in the "trusted advisor" driver's seat."

Omar Barraza, Marketing Expert, Founder of PlanStartGrow™, and creator of Almost Free Marketing™

"Kim's book is the most effective manifesto for revealing the intrinsic value of genuinely understanding a person's professional and personal needs, wants, and expectations. And while her book is destined to become a 'best seller' among resourceful sales professionals, I think it is a 'must read' for anyone in marketing interested in finding new ways to communicate more precisely, accurately, and effectively with past, present and future customers and clients. That's why we now incorporate the principles of Kim's innovative creation when introducing Almost Free Marketing™ and advise our clients to leverage Visnostic Statements too."

Pamela Luke, MBA, Sales and Marketing Professional

"This powerful book is chock-full of brilliant non-conventional sales and marketing advice on so many levels. One point of value applicable to many industries is the marketing team may never be in a position to purchase the product their company manufactures. Yet, they are required to produce material that will capture the market. This requires a combination of ingenuity and great salesmanship to clinch the deal. Kim takes the reader seamlessly through the steps

needed to make the "sell" genuine in order to win while offering positive and engaging motivation."

**Commander Cynthia O'Neil & Lieutenant Brandon O'Neil
Senior Buyers for the Fort Worth Police Department**

"Personally having no distinct sales background in marketing or technology, a company recently came in to present their offering of an internet platform they built to show how it could improve work in my field, as I represented a local municipality. I was interested in the concept and eager to see if I thought their product could improve our data collection, as were fifteen other decision makers sitting in the room. Five minutes after they started their PowerPoint presentation I thought to myself "I'm not engaged in this. I do not see why it is important to have this". Ten minutes later looking around the room multiple others had begun checking their phones or otherwise checking out. I had recently read a draft of Kim's book and had multiple conversations with her on Visnostic Statements and the benefits of engaging listeners (clients) in visualization and true feedback. As a consumer or customer I feel I have a better understanding of what to expect from a product or sales meeting and if the person who says they can provide it, really understands my needs and how their product can fulfill them.

I wish this company had read this book or spoken with Kim on truthfully and honestly engaging with the client or end user to prepare their presentation. The presenter did have a valid product they were trying to bring to the market but most likely could have improved market buy in thousands of times faster and more successfully if they had the knowledge this author or her methods bring to the table."

Bridget Cogley, Tableau Zen Master & Visualization Expert

"We can automate so much. What we can't automate is the human connection, the relationships we build and the novel - and very human - solutions we improvise. Kimberlee understands this, humanizing data and using it to find success in a manner that proves itself time and time again. So, use it to change sales, but use it elsewhere too. Where do you need to build connection and convince others?

Visnostic Selling gets to the heart of what clients want - not just what businesses want to throw at them. It lets prospects share their values, deepest dreams, and hopes, so that you - a fellow human - can bond and see a shared path in a way that no automation can provide. You know the potential solution and path your business can provide. What's often missing are the unique gaps clients see, fear, and want to correct. Kimberlee provides a system that's human-centric, allowing us to bypass jargon that's cluttered the path to understanding to get to the root of what clients need. It builds success in a way that's transformational, sustainable, and wildly successful.

Use this book to bond and to transform the process so the client shines, you support them on their path, and trust becomes the norm. Expand by letting this process become a longitudinal benchmark, allowing you to return, re-prioritize, and reach new heights with clients. Intuition and data-driven decision-making can work together."

Carolynn Boss, Senior Vice President of Sales and Business Development

"Having been in Sales more than half of my career, I wish that someone had shared this unique way of approaching a client before. I've been successful in my career but I could have done so much more. So many times I was forced to use the Company presentation that spent 30-60 minutes bragging about the size and importance of the company I was working for and then went into deep heavy duty product descriptions that could literally put a client to sleep. Visualization Diagnostic Statements allows the client to be able to understand the benefits he would derive from your technology, understand how it will help his company (and even his career progression when he makes a great decision), while creating an almost automatic sponsor for you while doing it. Sometimes we just need to dare to be different. I find myself looking for the Visualization Diagnostic Statements that should be used for every sales conversation now."

Kelly, Account Representative, Ad Agency ($697 Million in annual revenue)

"The concept of Visnostic Statements has truly revolutionized the way I help my clients develop messaging for their brand. Kim's workshop encouraged my clients to recognize the importance of adopting a customer-centric strategy, which will help their brand resonate with prospective customers and ultimately increase sales of their products."

Harrison, Regional Sales Manager for Fortune 100 Company

"Kim's Visualization Diagnostic Statements will give my team of new sellers a scientific method for how to create content &

communicate their company's value to customers. The power in Kim's methodology for my team comes from its simplicity, relatability & ease of deployment in their day-to-day.

As a management tool it helps to show where each reps' strengths & weaknesses are so I can continue to develop my people as effectively as possible. Thanks to Kim, my team & I will be more confident in communicating our value to customers."

Lynda Stokes, Politician and Former Mayor of Reno, TX

"Kimberlee Slavik Has done a masterful job in explaining the art of communication/sales through neuroscience.

Reading her book is as easy as having coffee with a friend. The stories in this book and the Individual exercises help us to better understand our own thought process in order to communicate with others. As a politician I know we have just a few seconds to grab someone's attention. Kim's book will help you break through the walls we all build.

In the business world I am constantly challenged to put myself out there as a product to others. This book is giving me insight and tools to build a vision and the ability to develop visions in others. Therefore, better fulfilling their needs.

Putting this into play can pull somebody from the bottom of the barrel and put them at the top of the mountain.

PREFACE

Introduction and Prerequisites
WHY/HOW/WHAT

WHY you want to read this book

Once upon a time, there was a mother and daughter. One gorgeous afternoon, these lovely women were carrying on a family tradition of cooking a prize-winning roast. The recipe was a closely guarded secret and had been in their family for decades. However, the recipe was extremely precise. The roast had to be an exact weight, the spices had to be carefully measured, the meat had to marinate for a specific amount of time, and even the weather had to be just right for the oven to work its magic.

One day as the mother was teaching all the secrets to the daughter, the roast was properly prepared and it was ready to be put into the pan. Suddenly, the mother pulled out a cutting board and cut the end of the roast off. The daughter was confused and asked the mother why she did that. The mother scratched her head and said, "I honestly don't know. This is how my mother taught me to do it. Let me call her and ask."

The mother called the matriarch and described how perfectly the roast preparation had gone and then asked for the reason they cut off the end of the roast before cooking. The elder mother burst out laughing and said, "Well Honey, I don't know why YOU did it but my pan was too small! "

I absolutely love this story because there is a little bit of this story in all of us. We tend to do things because it was the way they were always done. Every once in a while, we will stop and ponder why we do it and if it can be done differently. If I could summarize this book, this is it. You are about to learn how to do something VERY unique!

In fact, you are about to embark on a journey that will change everything you thought you knew about marketing and sales. Once you have finished this book, you will be armed with powerful knowledge and insight that will inspire you to do things very differently from the way you do them today. You will want to review and enhance your current messaging which will make it much more meaningful, impactful, and memorable to your audience. It will also change the way you purchase things because your expectations will change with how you view a sales process.

Your message will be reconstructed to inspire your audience. You will transform your presentations with less words and better visuals to ensure your audience remembers your message. They will want to engage with you and share important strengths and weaknesses with you. You will be amazed as your audience becomes enthusiastic about what you have to offer them and their company.

> **" People don't just buy from people they like. They buy because they become emotional about the potential solutions and the people from whom they buy.**

You will experience for yourself how one simple word can trigger many different emotions and visualizations. Knowing and seeing this will help you ensure you validate your audiences' interpretations of your words. You will become aware of how our brains avoid work and how this avoidance keeps sales and clients out of sync with one another. However, you will also learn how to ensure this isn't a problem in the future.

You will learn the importance of translating your offerings into a language and delivery to which your clients can relate. You will see how this translation step strengthens your relationship with your clients because they will be grateful that you will take this translation burden off their shoulders. You will learn how to take data from your clients and translate it into valuable information that they can use to sell you and your capabilities internally. You will learn how to create your own tools that will aid in translating pains, weaknesses, challenges, and strengths into an insightful and powerful deliverable for your client. Subsequently, you will change your life, your clients' lives, and the lives of the people around you with this new knowledge and skill!

> **❝❝**You will change your life, your clients' lives, and the lives of the people around you with this new knowledge and skill!

WHY & HOW this book is written

RUSSIAN NESTING DOLLS

Simon Sinek's book *Start With Why* is one of the most watched Ted Talks of all time with millions of views, and dozens of spin-offs. Sinek created a drawing of three circles with "Why" being the middle starting point. He explains that most companies go right into WHAT they do but they should really start by explaining, "WHY they do what they do." A company should begin each presentation with the purpose and motivation behind what they believe.

The second outer circle should address their process and explain the specific actions they take to support the "WHY." This second step answers HOW they will do what they do.

Finally, the outer most circle and third step should explain WHAT they do. This is when the result of the WHY is explained. Simon Sinek refers to these three steps as "The Golden Circles." However, when the artist of this book saw the circles, he envisioned that those circles were an aerial view of a Russian Nesting Doll.

For those who don't know what that is, it is a small doll that fits inside a medium doll, that fits inside a large doll. Because visualizations are a critical part of neuroscience, this graphic should help you remember the order in which this thought process flows: Why, How, and What.

I will attempt to follow Simon Sinek's thought process and this preface will explain **WHY** I am writing this book, **WHY** you will want to read it, **HOW** you can maximize your benefits and retention of the content, **HOW** you will execute, and **WHAT** you can do to immediately increase your income.

While this is intended to be a stand-alone reference guide, there are some prerequisite research materials that will help you be much more passionate about what you are about to learn. In order to truly appreciate and comprehend the content, it will be incredibly helpful for you to understand the basics of Sinek's *Start With Why* because it is full of fundamental details about how the brain works chemically.

After you finish that research, look into *The Challenger Sale* by Matthew Dixon and Brent Adamson, which does an incredible job of explaining why most sales people never get that important second meeting. It also teaches how your customers need you to communicate with them in order to bring value to your meetings.

Clients want you to paint a vision of how their lilfe and company could be better in the future with your help.

It also does a fantastic job explaining why relationship selling (alone) is not as impactful as previously taught and how to address that so it is actually the most impactful sales approach when combined with the Challenger style.

Finally, please read *What Great Salespeople Do* by Michael Bosworth and Ben Zoldan. It basically explains why *The Bible* is the best selling book of all times; it is full of stories, and our brains LOVE stories! It teaches how to craft your stories in order to maximize the impact on your audience. Bosworth's book made so many light bulbs go off in my head that it was blinding. **I finally understood the science behind some of the strange things I had to do to get my clients to understand how I was going to help them.**

All three of these recommended books are incredible reading by themselves; however, when you put all three together, they describe the most powerful communication approach that I have ever seen.

> 🖌🖌 **Paint a vision of how their life and company could be better in the future with your help.**

Neuroscience is not just beneficial during a sales process; it is also useful in all the relationships in your life. But the value I want to provide to each reader is a detailed description of specific ways you can take the science described, convert what marketing has already created for you, and go deliver the message in a way that your clients want and need you to deliver it!

For those of you who haven't read these books or have a light background in basic sales psychology, please refer to Appendix for some fundamental information that you will want to know.

WHY this book has more graphics and fewer words than most business books

While the average business book has over 70,000 words and few graphics, each of my books will have less than 30,000 words and several dozen graphics. **Why** am I doing that? Because I want every reader to actually finish reading the entire contents in one sitting AND the pictures will help readers remember the content!

Did you know what our attention spans are getting shorter? In 2000, you had twelve seconds to keep my attention. Today, you only have eight seconds! To put that into perspective, a gold fish has a nine second attention span. That means that a gold fish will pay attention longer than a human today! I have worked with enough sales people to tell you that I highly suspect the typical sales person has an even lower attention span than a typical human!

I once read that a study was conducted on college students attending the same class, learning from the same books, the same instructor, and taking the same tests. However, one group did better than the other. The only difference was that one group attended classes Monday, Wednesday, and Friday for one hour each day. The other group attended Tuesday and Thursday for one hour and thirty minutes each day. The conclusion of the study was that the shorter the instruction, the better the retention. I'm not sure if this is true of not, but it's another data point to support my strategy of using less words.

"You are Who You Are, Because of Where You Were, When" is one of my all time favorite quotes. I recommend that you familiarize yourself with this concept. Entire books have been written on this subject so we won't be able to spend much time dissecting it. However, understanding this concept will enhance your ability to have empathy for your audience. If you understand the basic concept and the importance of adapting to your audience, you will be even better at learning this new communication process. Here is a URL to help you quickly grasp the primary points of this theory https://www.youtube.com/watch?v=_aY163kwIW4.

From my perspective, I love to learn and I love to try new things. Therefore, throughout my career I embraced the latest sales training that came out. While each book or training course was incredible, and I always learned something new from each one, I also scratched my head in bewilderment. Don't writers know that most sales people have an incredibly short attention span? Why are books so long? And why are they full of so much 'filler'? When am I supposed to have time to read all these books? Do publishers demand a certain number of pages or words to legitimize the content?

Well, here is the reality of MY world as an eager reader and student

– I would get a new book, enthusiastically start reading and by about the fifth chapter, life disrupted my reading and I had to put down the book. A few days or even weeks later, when I got back to the book, I would feel the need to scan the first chapters again to get my head back in the game.

I have dozens of business books in my office and even more audio books on various devices. I bet I have read or listened to the first five chapters dozens of times. Sadly, I usually finished them only once! I'm embarrassed to admit this, but I am pretty sure that I have a couple of fantastic books that I never even finished! So why do that to someone else?

The goal is that with less than 30,000 words, you will read each of my books in one sitting; this should increase the probability that you take your excitement and execute while it is fresh in your memory. In fact, I plan on having you execute in Chapter ONE so not only will you see first hand the power of neuroscience, you will have the confidence to do it TODAY! I also want you to believe in what you are reading. The exercises are critical so you can see these concepts work instantly. As each point is proven to you, you will become more passionate about leveraging these new skills immediately.

WHY exercises will help you learn and retain and execute more effectively

Most of you have probably seen versions of this graphic throughout your career. Which means you all should know that your ability to retain what you learn is maximized when you 'teach' the materials. Therefore, as you read, you will notice multiple exercises that are intended to simulate a teaching scenario that will enhance your comprehension.

Unfortunately, per neuroscience and human nature, you will be tempted to skip the exercises. Despite the fact that doing the exercises with other people will increase your ability to remember and comprehend the content, you will convince yourself that you are special and don't need this enhancement for adequate learning. Fight this urge!

Why waste your time reading this book if you only retain 10% of what you read? Doing each exercise will ensure you not only read, but also, hear, see, discuss, experience, and teach. By retaining 95% of what is in the book, you will not waste your valuable time reading a book that you won't remember and you will be more prepared to actually execute these powerful new skillsets!

WHY Graphics are powerful

I also want to explain **why** there is a need for so many graphics. As I shared a draft of this book, I was thrilled how many people gave feedback by referring to the graphics associated with the content. Graphics help the reader retain the information! Take a look at your current presentations. Do you have more words than pictures? Do your graphics compliment your words? If not, this needs to change immediately. When graphics and words don't compliment each other, it confuses the audience. This confusion will cause them to disengage.

Recently I read an article on LinkedIn by Inc. called **"7 Presentation Ideas That Work for Any Topic."** https://www.inc.com/carmine-gallo/7-presentation-ideas-that-work-for-any-topic.html

First of all, I agree with every single word in this article, but I questioned the author as I read it because it instructed the reader to use more pictures than words. Yet there were no pictures. It said to avoid bullets but each point was numbered AND there were bullets. In my opinion, a bullet and a number are the same thing. This made the article seem somewhat hypocritical to me and it is important that I don't do that to my readers. My point here is that I am going to teach you how to do things and I am going to "lead by example" as much as possible. In fact, if you catch me falling short, be sure to communicate your observations with me so I can fix it in future releases! It is so easy to read HOW to do something, but it is a much bigger challenge to go out there and actually execute what you learned!

❝❝ How can an author legitimize the content if the advice is not followed during the instruction?

Therefore, you will notice that almost every page will have at least one photo or graphic highlighting a point made in the content. This serves multiple purposes. I want you to remember the content but I also want you to find what you are looking for when you need to go back and reference, re-read, or find something.

❝❝ These points are not intended to instruct you how I am writing a book; they are intended to inspire you to follow this same logic when creating communications with your clients.

I have so many random facts in my head, yet I am challenged to remember who said it or from what book it came. My goal is that while you visualize the artwork, you will remember the content, and be able to quickly reference what you need in the future. Furthermore, as I travel, teach, and present this methodology, the graphics will replace most of the words and become the focal point of my presentation to improve retention of the content.

" Visualization is a major part of the power of neuroscience.

You will also notice repetition as you read. Studies have uncovered that the mind has to absorb information multiple times and multiple ways to comprehend and retain the concept. So if you find yourself reading something familiar yet a little different, this has been done intentionally to help you retain the content.

The importance of two-way communications in presentations

As you look at these two drawings, imagine you are one of the characters in each scene. Which drawing seems to represent the most pleasant form of communication? Do you prefer to be in listen mode or do you prefer to be engaged in the communication process? Pause as you look at these two scenes and dissect why you chose one over the other. Why is two-way communication so much more attractive than one-way communication? Why do some people struggle with reading? Which scene is most like reading a book? Isn't reading like being in listening mode? Why do we need classrooms if we can just read books and learn the content?

Have you ever read an interactive book? I don't think I have! I am sure they exist but they are most certainly in short supply. This is interesting because we are taught in neuroscience that one-way communications are not stimulating and they are unnatural.

Therefore, I will be asking you to do some exercises and email me your stories. This may seem like a silly thing to do, but it will help you retain what you learned. It will also help you to visualize the emotions you just witnessed. It will be a good experience for you so you will be prepared to convert these approaches to your work life because the ultimate goal is that you will increase your pipeline immediately.

❝❝ How much you get out of this book is up to you and is dependent upon how well you follow these instructions.

WHAT are Visualization Diagnostic Statements™?

NOTE - Also referred to as a VDS, Diagnostic Statement, or Visnostic in this book.

A Visnostic or Visualization Diagnostic Statement are trademarked terms created by Kimberlee Slavik, CEO of DynaExec. It is a statement that requires a response from an audience. It stimulates emotional responses inspiring your audience to maximize their interest in your message. Visualization Diagnostic Statement is the scientific term. However, readers may want to refer to it by a term more in alignment with their specific business and client base.

The statements typically **translate** features and functions into something more meaningful to the audience.

A Visnostic Statement often originates as an ineffective, generic, one-way **self-focused** message that has been converted into a meaningful two-way engaging statement that is **audience-focused**. Existing presentations, brochures, case studies, and other marketing materials are often reworded to become Visnostic Statements.

A Visnostic Statement is also a qualification tool that will help you assess your audience. As you go through the statements, if your participant isn't responding or is struggling with responding, chances are high that you aren't in front of the right participant.

A Visnostic Statement is also an effective way to determine if sales and marketing currently have the right messaging. If creating these statements feels effortless, the current messaging is strong. When these statements are difficult to create, the content doesn't contain what the clients need and want to know.

The Importance of A Diagnostic Approach
Cause versus Symptom

I recently participated in a group interview for a sales leadership role. Several people described things they saw as broken in the sales organization and they asked me how I would fix these problems. The complaints ranged from sales were down to morale was low. My response to them was that they were describing a symptom and asking me how to eliminate the pain before I understood the cause of that pain. For my response, I used the analogy of a headache and how a physician would handle a patient with the same dilemma.

Prescribing a painkiller to help the headache go away will not address the cause of the pain; it will only temporarily mask the symptom. I continued by explaining that multiple things could cause a headache such as allergies, caffeine withdrawal, vision problems, medications, a hangover, hormones, a brain tumor, just to name a few. Yet each cause of these pains must be treated very differently in order to eliminate the pain.

Just as a good doctor will dig deeper and run tests to determine the cause of the pain, a good salesperson or sales leader should also investigate to ensure he or she is addressing the correct cause of the issues. For example, I typically interview people, review reports, analyze the competitive marketplace, and examine existing business tools in order to uncover the cause of the problem. Too often enthusiastic and new sales professionals will start attempting to fix the symptom versus taking the necessary extra time to uncover the cause of the issues. This happens with internal pains as well as client pains.

Not until a successful diagnosis of the **cause** of the pain is made, can the appropriate plan of action be executed to eliminate the **source** of the pain.

Visnostic Statements should be constructed to identify your clients' pains and the cause of their pains. It is the responsibility of the sales organization to differentiate pains, challenges, and weaknesses as either causes or symptoms.

Converting typical sales points into this unique format will engage your client and create the desire to share important details that will help properly diagnose the cause and how the client can be helped.

Why This Is Relevant and Important
If a salesperson is taught a presentation and delivers the presentation on sales calls, do they really understand the client's source of the pain?

Converting presentations into "Visnostic Statements" is the first step in creating a powerful tool that will help diagnose the most effective areas in which the sales team can help the client. Visnostic Statements will create an environment that will stimulate meaningful and valuable conversations with the client.

WHAT This Book Is NOT

I originally wrote this book to replace a traditional resumé. However, as I shared drafts of this book, people immediately started asking me to come speak to their teams and help them execute the principles of this book.

While this response was exciting, the objective is that I provide enough information that each reader can perform these communication skills without any additional assistance from me. However, I also want each reader to be successful with these principals so if you struggle, please reach out for help. **While it may sound like it at times, the book is not intended to be a sales pitch for using any of my services or the services of any other company mentioned.**

WHAT Buyers Learn

I knew this book would benefit sales professionals, marketing teams, sales leaders, and any other client-facing roles in an organization. I never envisioned that BUYERS would find the content of value. However, as I was having close friends and family review the draft, I received some unexpected feedback from two people with zero sales backgrounds. While they didn't sell for a living, they did have frequent purchasing requirements and were often forced to endure some pretty tough and painful sales presentations.

I was excited to hear that a few weeks after reading a draft, a very important sales presentation was conducted. People that had a vested interest in learning more about the offering attended the meeting. These two people just happened to be in the same presentation and they told me they viewed the sales people very differently after learning about the concepts around Visnostic Statements.

They explained that they were on opposite sides of the room, texting each other about how horrible the slides were. They were full of words and bullets and had very few graphics that made sense. They looked around the room and observed the entire audience was disengaged and on their various smart devices. The sales people had lost the interest of the entire room and now my two friends understood why the presentation was not effective!

These two people went on to explain that they are stronger and more educated buyers after reading the draft. They continued explaining that their expectations are higher than they were before reading the book. They also suggested that I reach out to the company that presented to them because they actually want to buy the offering. However, the sales people simply didn't build a strong enough case to justify the purchase! This is such terrific insight from Buyers! Therefore, try and imagine how your clients would react to the content you are reading. What would YOUR clients say about YOUR interaction with them?

WHAT to Expect

As you begin reading, you should notice two very distinct styles of writing. Chapters one through three will focus on creating or converting one-way communications into an audience-centric message that will be more powerful and produce better results. These chapters tend to be more internally focused. Depending on your organization, marketing may be more involved with these first three chapters because of the focus on the content and structure of the message.

Chapters four through five are more focused on client interactions, gathering client data, and converting this client feedback into valuable information. You may find the need to bring in more technical team members to create your company's tool when you get to this point of the book.

During the review of the draft, most sales people found the first three chapters to be very creative and visionary. The last two chapters were found to be more difficult because they require more technical knowledge. I encourage all readers to remember that it is the combination of these two styles that will produce results that are significant for both sales and clients.

VDS are Universally Effective

Even though my career has been primarily associated with Silicon Valley companies, Visnostic Statements should apply to all sales scenarios. For example, if you are a realtor and you sell houses based upon number of bedrooms, bathrooms, square footage, and price, you will sell more if you lead with the real reason clients actually buy homes. One of the greatest realtors I ever worked with told me that she didn't sell homes; she sold dreams. Creating effective VDS will flush out those dreams.

I'm also working with a paint company that insists their buyers buy on price and relationships. They believe that all of their Buyers consider paint to be a commodity. My response to this comment was, **"If your clients view your offerings as a commodity, you are SELLING it as a commodity; VDS will highlight the differentiators that will help change this perspective."**

To summarize this introduction, you now know WHY this book was written, why you should follow the instructions, and why it is formatted in an unusual way. You also now understand HOW to get the most out of what you read, and WHAT the outcome should be for you, your company, and your clients.

WARM UP EXERCISE

Use this space to summarize your interpretation of this drawing. After completing the reading, you will reflect again to see how it has changed.

CHAPTER ONE

Believing is doing

The Birth of Visualization Diagnostic Statements

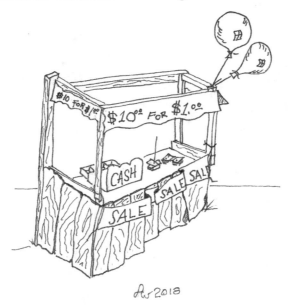

Aw 2018

In 2004 I represented a company and a service that I was so passionate about that I invested in the company. I sincerely believed that I had ten-dollar bills for sale for just one dollar.

Think about that! If someone gave you a stack of ten-dollar bills and told you that they would pay you commissions to go sell them for one dollar, wouldn't you call every person you knew? Wouldn't you jump out of bed in the morning and go on sales calls with tremendous enthusiasm? I was setting up at least five meetings each day and I would have done more but I ran out of daylight. I still hold sales records at that company! That was my life for the first decade of my

1

career and I sincerely believed that my customers loved me for educating them on what I was selling.

However, there was this one client that shocked and frustrated me because he didn't seem to see the value I brought to him and his company. This is the story of how Visualization Diagnostic Statements were born.

The first time I presented to him, he fell asleep. HE FELL ASLEEP! Of course he was embarrassed and set up another meeting. I was actually encouraged during the second meeting because I noticed him taking very vigorous notes. He seemed to be really concentrating and really into what he was writing down. I walked over to him and he was doing his grocery list. HE WAS DOING HIS GROCERY LIST!

shopping list

produce	dairy	dry
apples	yogurt	peanut butter
bananas	butter	canned tomato
lemons	eggs	pasta
spinach	kefer	black beans
kale		
celery		
cucumber	meat	misc
yams.	chicken	t.p.
red onion		la croix
garlic		laundry det.

I was young and so bewildered that someone wasn't paying attention to me! After all, I WAS SELLING TEN DOLLAR BILLS FOR JUST ONE DOLLAR! I had lost him for the second time and I was frustrated because I had been working with him for a year. Of course I KNEW he would love me for what I could do for him! How could he not want to pay attention to what I had to say?

I actually stopped the presentation and pleaded with him to tell me what I was doing wrong. He said nothing was wrong. He then stated that he had to be honest with me; he didn't have a budget to buy anything so he was just meeting with me to be nice.

At that moment, I knew I had to approach things very differently for him to digest how I could rock his world with my service. He told me that he was sorry that he wasted my time. I thanked him for his honesty and I left but I didn't stop thinking about what he said and what I did NOT say.

One of my personal mottos was "No" means "Try Harder." So I accepted the fact that I was accountable for this failure because I was doing something ineffective and I needed to try harder, or in this case try something different.

I was convinced that my presentation just wasn't keeping his attention. I thought of all the things that I should have said to him while I was there. My software didn't need a budget because the return on investment was extremely high and it was fast.

How could I go back to him and deliver this message differently? How could I get him to listen to me? I don't know how I came up with this idea. I don't think I am that smart so it must have been some type of divine intervention. I took my slide deck and for the first time, I really dissected what each bullet said. Why wasn't this working? It was the same deck I used to sell everybody else so why didn't this guy get excited too?

I tried to put myself in his shoes and read my presentation through his eyes. I never really looked at my messaging through my clients' eyes. I always viewed my presentation as MY story and MY COMPA-NY's story. I suddenly realized that each bullet sounded so generic. I sounded like each of my competitors. I sounded like I could have been selling anything.

I then reviewed our other marketing tools such as brochures, web pages, advertisements, infographics, and anything else I could find that explained what we did for our clients.

I reworded each marketing point and instead of approaching the communication with "this is what WE can do for you," I changed the wording to be a statement that HE would make.

When I first created these statements, I called them "Challenge Statements." However, when I started to document my experiences, I researched that term. I discovered that the definitions and descriptions were an established legal term. This did not align with what I was doing. I worried that referring to these phrases as Challenge Statements would cause too much confusion. So I changed the term to "Diagnostic Statements" but quickly discovered this was also an established term used in nursing. It is because of these past name changes that, "Visualization Diagnostic Statements" has been trademarked. While this current term better describes the science behind what is accomplished, unfortunately it was a mouthful and difficult to say. Therefore, by combining Visualization and Diagnostics, the word, Visnostics was born and trademarked!

I am explaining this because in a few pages, you will see a copy of the original document. I want to avoid any confusion the different terms may cause the readers. Challenge Statements, Visnostic Statements, Diagnostic Statements, Visualization Diagnostic Statements, and VDS are the same thing. Both the name and the process have evolved through the years.

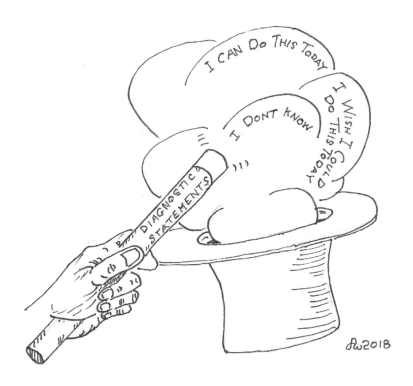

I then made four columns in a Word document. I labeled these columns "Would like to say this," "Say this today," "NA, Not important, or do not know" and "Challenge Statement." Next, I took each presentation bullet of the features/functions/benefits of what I was selling and made each bullet a line item. Once this new document was completed, I called the client back and asked him to go to lunch with me. At first he resisted and reminded me that he didn't have a budget and wasn't going to buy from me. I reassured him that I heard that message loud and clear in our meeting, but I really needed a favor. I promised not to try selling him anything. I just needed his advice on how I could do things better in the future. I explained that I had created a new tool that I wanted to share and listen to his valuable feedback. Once he knew I wasn't trying to sell him, he agreed to lunch. I suspect there may even be a chapter in neuroscience about our eagerness to respond when someone needs our help.

Once we were at lunch and had our food, I pushed my plate aside. I apologized to him for trying to force a presentation. I explained that this time I had a different approach that didn't require a projector, conference room, or even a laptop. All I had was a piece of paper with printing on one side. I told him that I was going to make a statement and with each statement, I would need him to respond with one of three responses. "I can do this today," "I wish I could do this today," or "I don't know, not important, not applicable."

NOTE: After reading this book, Bosworth began referring to these client responses as "AFFIRMATIONS" and he actually wrote about these affirmations in the Foreword. However, be careful not to confuse the client affirmations with the actual statements. A statement is always a statement even after the client responds, but not all client responses will be affirmations. For example, if a client responds to the statement, "not important" or "not applicable," the client response is NOT an affirmation. However, the statement is still a statement. This is an important principle to understand while reading this book.

He agreed and I started with the first line. "Restore is a simple and visual process." His eyes immediately looked up and to the left; I was stunned. I had been taught that sales people should look for this body language because it meant that the audience was envisioning something that would get them emotionally engaged in the conversation.

To my surprise, not only did he say he WISHED he could do that today, he elaborated on how they did it today and how long it took and how painful it was. He even told me a story about how the CEO had accidentally deleted an email. The CEO frantically called the IT department and explained that this was an emergency and he needed them to restore that email immediately.

However, it took over twenty-four hours to find the back up of the deleted email and restore it. In fact, someone had actually been terminated because it took so long to restore. He explained that the inability of the IT Department to restore lost data in a timely manner was now extremely visible at the CEO level and the IT department was now considered to be incompetent at the highest level within the company.

Wow! That was some valuable information about the "pain" he was feeling in his current role.

I restored the original document I designed in 2004 so I could include a copy to share here. I did edit it and took out all references to what company this was, the competitors, and specific shared applications names that were needed. It's important to share because it looks primitive, ugly, and very simplistic, but it was so much more effective than my gorgeous, fifty slides, professionally crafted presentation that the company provided to me.

As you can tell from the Challenge Statement column, I was selling business continuity software. However, no need to spend any time trying to read the details in the "Statement" section because the details are not important. Just know that each statement started out as a bullet in a presentation; this was the same presentation during which this client fell asleep and wrote his grocery list!

The reality is that the client doesn't care about all the cosmetics if you can't get him/her engaged in the content and have an intelligent, two-way dialogue.

❝❝ If the client isn't talking, the salesperson isn't learning how to help the client!

I realize that this sounds so logical and simple. However, all sales professionals know just how difficult it can be to get clients to share information. And now we know WHY — "The Fight or Flight" instinct is a powerful adversary during each sales cycle.

The secret to overcoming this response is to get them emotionally, not just intellectually, engaged. **Creating effective Visnostic Statements and asking them to reflect and respond is the tactical instruction that has been missing from every sales methodology book that I have read.** This is why this process is unique and like nothing you have ever read until now.

It's important to understand that this isn't a theory or hypothesis. It is a methodology that I have been utilizing for over ten years and it has worked at multiple companies with different products and services.

It is also an approach that none of my clients have ever seen another salesperson do. It is a universal technique and since nobody is doing it, it will be refreshing to your clients when you approach them with this new communication style. That is, until the lessons taught in this book become normal business practice.

Here is a pasted version of the very simple document that I created over ten years ago. This process has evolved but I will help you with the basics first and then I will explain some enhancements that have been added through the years. As you can see, it doesn't have to be pretty to be effective.

Company Name:
Date: 2004
Because the XYZ solution is very robust, and we have a limited amount of time to demonstrate the software, please take a moment to answer the following questions so our presentation can be customized for you and your company.

1. Attendees

Name	Title	Function

2. Specific "Deleted" Concerns - What are THREE "challenges" that you are tasked with or most concerned about?

Name	Challenge #1	Challenge #2	Challenge #3
	Compliancy	No budget	With (competitors name) today

3. Please put a check mark next to one of the three options describing your current situation with back-up and restore

Would LIKE to say this	SAY this TODAY	NA, Not Important or do not know (?)	Challenge Statement
✓			Restore is a simple and visual process
	✓		Quickly and easily find and restore missing files
✓			Avoid wasteful and costly differential back-up jobs
✓			In seconds, scroll back in time to view past server state
✓			Missing files and directories are seen as conspicuous cross-hatched objects and a single click launches the restore job
	✓		Reduce hardware costs by exploiting inexpensive serial ATA-devices.
			Decrease backup time
✓			Ultra quick restores from disk
✓			Integrate Disk-to-Disk-to-Tape with Synthetic Full Backup to maximize benefits.
		N/A	Backup time shrinks drastically
✓			Only incremental backups are needed. (XYZ performs full back-ups1x wk)
✓			Reduce network traffic by only sending incremental data over the LAN.
✓			Restore time is optimized since restore is from the synthetic full job on disk/tape.
✓			Potentially run incremental backups forever and synthetic fulls.
✓			Avoid wasteful and costly differential back-up jobs
	✓		Create offsite tapes during your regular, nightly backups
✓			Simultaneously write to disk and tape
✓			Save time by not having to re-run backups or having to duplicate tapes during the day.
✓			The ability to backup through a single port created as a secure outbound connection.
✓			No open (inbound) ports are needed for backup
	✓		The ability to restart a job from the point of failure
		?	The ability to pause an active job midstream?
		?	Failed backup jobs over the LAN can be automatically restarted and pick-up from where they left off and not restart the job over from the beginning
	✓		Pause and restart an active job at any time for any reason
		?	Ability to restore your own data through a web browser
		?	Personalize XML-based reports
✓			Align costs with SLAs
✓			Vendor appreciates you and treats you as a valued partner

About half way through the list of my Visnostic Statements, he pushed his plate of food aside and he commented that he assumed my company could do all this or we wouldn't be going through this exercise. I said that was correct. He then asked me why the heck I didn't tell him this before now!

I looked him straight in the eyes and told him that this is the presentation that I gave him TWICE! **He laughed and said none of it even sounded familiar to him.**

> **This is when I realized that the presentation put too much stress on my client to translate or interpret the words on the slides.**

This new way of presenting the same information was allowing me to guide him through the thought process by eliminating the translation requirement. The result was that instead of dumping everything I could do for my client in a presentation and depending on him to translate, I was able to guide him to his own conclusion.

> **The client came to his own conclusion versus me telling him what to think. When it is his or her idea, they will become more receptive.**

He then asked if I could send an electronic version of this new document, including his responses, to him by close of business that same day! I said of course! I left the meeting and typed it all up, along with some of his commentary, which I had written on the back of this paper.

He called me the next day with questions. He confessed that he edited the document and was presenting it to the CEO as his own research with a recommendation to go with us to fix specific problems that would address the restoration delays the CEO had witnessed.

Within a month of this lunch, the deal closed and it made my number for the entire year. This was a client that had no budget and obviously no interest in my presentation because **his mind was on his own problems, not what my company had to say about ourselves.** Aren't most clients having this same experience when we take their valuable time?

❝❝ My content was exactly the same. The only difference was the way in which the content was communicated.

I felt like I had just invented the light bulb with this new approach! "No" means "Try Harder" or in this case, "No" meant that I needed to try something different.

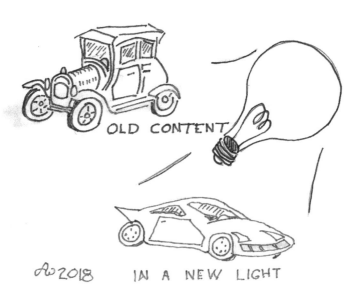

OLD CONTENT

A2018   IN A NEW LIGHT

This was when I realized that **HOW you articulate your message is more important than the actual content!** And this was over 10 years ago. I was never sure why this worked or what to call it. Today, it is called Neuroscience.

Since 2004, I have been converting presentation bullets into this format and taking this approach with my clients with huge success. This methodology has even evolved into something more powerful. Today, when a client responds with "I can do or say this today," I now ask him to grade himself with a one through five rating system. The scoring goes like this; if the client gives himself a one, that means they can do it but they have a lot of room for improvement. If the client scores himself a five, it means that he can do it today and he views it as perfect.

Now that you know the history of Visualization Diagnostic Statements as well as some of its evolution over the past decade, let's review some basic neuroscience that you will soon observe first hand. I am confident that each reader will be amazed to find this part of the book to be enlightening and fun.

Fun facts about how your brain works

3 CANDLES   3 MICE

3 PEAKS

The Power of THREEs

You are about to have your first experience with executing neuroscience exercises. Some of the exercises will go extremely well while others will have some challenges and may not even work at all. But don't be discouraged. Activities before and during the learning process will increase your retention of the content. After you read the entire book, go back and retry the exercises to see how much you have improved. It will be a great opportunity to see your progress while you evaluate your understanding of this new approach. It will also build your confidence that you are ready to execute with your clients.

There are so many books out today about neuroscience, which is basically a cool new buzzword for psychology. One of the points I read recently about neuroscience is to engage with your clients as soon as possible, which is why Chapter One starts with some executable exercises for the reader.

I also attended a leadership conference for women recently that taught the audience about the male brain preferring to have selections in groups of threes. To prove her point, the speaker showed us advertisements for three different tires. The speaker also told us that men prefer three colors of pants in their wardrobe: black, khaki, and blue. She supported these claims by having the only six men in the audience come on stage and she was correct; they all had on those colors of pants. These two simple new things I learned, helped validate why what I am about to share with you really does work and it works well!

The point of this story is to help you understand why I have three exercises for you to do in Chapter One, why you will see other topics in this book developed in sets of three. Per the aforementioned facts, at least fifty percent of our population prefers choices in threes or odd numbers. But I actually think the percentage is much higher.

3 CANDLES

The points made about men's brains reminded me of a woman's decorating class that taught that we think we want symmetrical settings, but our brain actual prefers things in uneven numbers. Therefore, it can be concluded that these preferences in groups of threes may apply to women as well as men.

Fight or Flight or Freeze

There are a few fundamental human instincts to keep in mind as you read the following directions. First of all, "fight or flight" is a real thing that haunts sales people. Humans have a natural instinct to put up walls, become defensive, or flee when someone is trying to sell to them, ask them for money, or persuade them. You don't believe this? When you see a sales call on your caller ID, do you enthusiastically answer your phone? When you answer the phone and it is a charity or sales person, do you hang up on them? Do you interrupt and tell them that you don't have time to talk? What other tactics to you use to avoid listening to them pitch to you? When you walk into a store, and a sales person asks if they can help you, do you attempt to brush them off by telling them that you are just looking?

As you read that there will be exercises, do you recall how that made you feel? Even if it occurred in your subconscious, my bet is that you already decided and JUSTIFIED why you don't need to do the exercises. Am I right? Humans are complex but we can be incredibly predictable as well.

Because I have been selling my entire career, you would think that I would be more receptive and patient with salespeople. However, I am far from it. I even took the time to add all of my numbers to the United States Do Not Call Registry.

The **Do Not Call Registry** accepts registrations from both cell phones and land lines. To **register** by telephone, **call** 1-888-382-1222 (TTY: 1-866-290-4236). You must **call** from the phone number that you want to **register**. To **register** online (**donotcall**.gov), you **will** have to respond to a confirmation email.

Sadly, it hasn't helped at all. Salespeople are annoying because our brains are wired to flee from persuasive scenarios. Those that force us to do things that are unnatural are difficult to trust.

❝❝ You are about to learn how to sell without getting the negative reaction that naturally occurs towards sales efforts.

Do Not Call

With the "Fight or Flight" instinct in mind, it is important that these exercises are not conducted without an explanation that will ensure that your participant's defensive walls are down. Please inform your participant that you are doing an experiment from a book you are reading. Then ask if they would please help you by participating by responding to a few statements.

Fight your Flight instincts and do these exercises!

The Power of Visualization

What does Visualization mean to you? Visualization is often described using several words like conversion, translation, interpretation, and envisioning. What if your vision is different than what your client is envisioning? Translating is hard work as well as risky because it can lead to misinterpretation. It is the biggest reason for lost sales and even lost clients.

A Different Type of Christmas Story

I want to share a story of a deal I lost due to two different visions of what my company could do for a client.

There was a time when companies needed to migrate data from one device to another device. In order to do this, companies had to bring down production to do a migration and holidays were a common time to do this due to low activity. I sold software that allowed companies to do this migration while production was live. Needless to say, this was a pretty easy sale.

I was in Dallas at a major retailers headquarters and I had already done a lot of homework. One of the men was a technical influencer and he mentioned to me that he hadn't been home with his family on Christmas Day in years. He explained that he would watch his children open their gifts and then head to the office for the rest of the day. I couldn't wait to give him the good news! He would never miss Christmas with his family ever again!

I thought I nailed the presentation! So you can imagine my shock at how quickly I was told that I would not be winning their business. I went back to their office to find out what I did wrong. To my surprise, the man that told me about working Christmas Day admitted that he killed the deal.

His reason was very simple. He relied very heavily on the triple pay he got on Christmas Day to buy the gifts for his family each year. Therefore, he viewed our services as a threat, not a benefit. When he told me that he hadn't been home in years, I interpreted that as a bad thing. I found out too late that he actually depended on it and there were other days he got extra pay that me and my company would eliminate. In other words, my offering hurt him and his family personally! This was a very painful lesson about the risk involved when translating sales benefits to client benefits. I would have bet my commission check that he viewed me as his HEROINE, not his VILLAIN!

There are at least two types of translation that take place during a sales cycle. Salespeople are trying to map their products and services to the pain and need of the client and the client is trying to interpret how the features and functions of the vendor's offering will convert to his or her world. This is a universal issue and yet we continue to handle it poorly.

❝❝ We need to take the translation risks out of the sales cycle.

Visualization Diagnostic Statements will flush out these important facts before you ever even present to your client!

EXERCISE #1
The Power of Visualization.

This is very simple to do and it works every single time!

In 2007, I was part of a transformation team that toured the country teaching "Order Takers" how to be "Hunters." I began my presentation with a little exercise that I want you to try before you read any further. I don't know where you are right now. You may be on a plane, or reading this in bed before you go to sleep, or on a lunch break. It doesn't matter where you are right now; what matters is that you have an innocent bystander that you can nab and ask him or her to participate in an exercise that will take less than 15 seconds. If you are alone, DO NOT be tempted to pick up the phone to call someone because it is important that you watch the participant's eyes. After you explain this is an experiment, just say these simple words –

"I am going to say a word and I need you to tell me the first VISUAL that pops into your head. What is the first thing you SEE when you hear this word...."

(Pause) Are you ready? (Pause)
"MONEY"

Be sure to carefully watch the eyes.

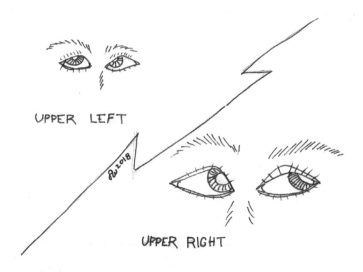

UPPER LEFT

UPPER RIGHT

The eyes will move rather fast so if you blink, you may miss it. Often, you will see them look up to the right or up to the left. As sales professionals, we should know the basics of body language and this means they are thinking and visualizing something. Ask them to be as detailed as possible when describing what they see. It's incredible how fast our minds visualize memories. Please send me an email describing what they say to you to this email address - money@dynaexec.com.

It is important that you follow these instructions because emailing me a description of what happened will help reinforce what you saw and learned. Those that skip this step will not improve as much as those that take time to reflect, envision, and document the observations of this exercise.

Lessons Learned From Exercise #1

There are so many lessons to be learned by doing this exercise.

One lesson is that our minds visualize things extremely fast when it is something to which we can relate.

Another lesson is that different minds process data differently. For example, I often get short answers during this exercise but every once in a while, a person will describe what sounds like a movie! Sometimes when I ask what a person visualizes, instead, they describe FEELINGS.

I was with a lady that I have hired three different times. She is the best sales person and relationship builder I have ever met. However, I consistently had challenges keeping her focused. I always assumed it was because she has been diagnosed with ADD. As we reviewed the draft of this book together, I became very aware that her brain moves faster and with many more details than other people. What she described to me when she heard the word "Money" was extremely emotional and thorough. She described money as being a source of freedom and then gave me multiple examples. The word triggered more emotions from her than any other person I have ever encountered. Her explanation went on for over ten minutes and her eyes were darting in every direction. I realized that not only did I get an understanding of how she views the word "money,' I also got an education on how different her thought process is compared to other people that have done this exercise with me. I was seeing first hand how difficult it is for a person with such an active brain to be focused on one thing at a time.

I realized that I needed to be aware of how her brain processes information and visualizes conversations so I can understand how I might want to adjust my own communication style with her. This will be enlightening as you get to know new clients as well. As she was talking, I wondered how many brains like hers have been diagnosed as having ADD when in reality their brains are much more active than other brains. To me, what I was witnessing was a gift or talent versus a handicap or disability as ADD is often viewed.

A few weeks later, I did this same exercise with a relative and she said she has so many negative feelings around the word money. She also went into great detail about the bad feelings that surfaced when she heard this word.

Words can trigger unexpected emotional responses.

Both of these ladies described **feelings** when they heard the word versus an **image**. One responded positively emotionally and the other responded negatively. The word was the same but the responses and perceptions were complete opposites. Why does this matter?

If you are presenting, you are assuming that your audience comprehends your message the way you intend it to be received. But how can you determine if you are accomplishing this goal? How do you determine how your client is processing information? Those that visualize a movie may have a more challenging time keeping up during a fast paced presentation. This reaction may cause you to lose important points with some members of your audience.

What if I told you that Visnostic Statements will ensure that your clients communicate their interpretation of your messaging? This will enable you to avoid miscommunication from occurring.

> **❝❝ Getting your audience to visualize and articulate their current situation is the most impactful way to get them emotionally engaged in your conversation while validating their comprehension of the points you are making.**

During this exercise, the more details your participant gives you, the more emotional engagement you will observe. The eyes will reveal additional emotions and you can observe the magnitude of the visualizations taking place in their mind.

Now let's discuss why most people will resist following the instructions around this exercise.

While writing and sharing with a test group, not one person followed the instructions or shared their experience with me via email as requested. This in itself is proof that when someone feels they are being coerced or persuaded to do something, the natural instinct is to rebel and flee. It was simply too much work for the reader. So why do we expect a different response from our clients? Translating is hard work. That makes it very risky for sales because it can lead to misinterpretations by your clients.

❝❝ The more work you do for the client, the more you will be perceived as adding value and the more receptive your client will be to your message.

I did this exercise with one of my favorite recruiters and she told me that she saw an orange. Because that was the first time I had ever heard that response, I asked her to elaborate on why she saw an orange. She explained that money buys her food and she loves oranges. So this conversation with my recruiter is even more evidence how one single word can mean so many different things to many different people. As sales people, one of our biggest challenges is to understand how our audience is interpreting our words.

❝❝ **Words translate differently because we each have different experiences. One single word can mean different things triggering completely different emotions within each person.**

I recall many conversations I have had with clients over the years where we had communication challenges because their interpretations of "the cloud" or "implementation" were very different than my company or mine. As I described in an earlier story, even working on Christmas Day can have different perspectives and produce different emotional responses. Understanding your client's unique visualizations will help you exceed versus falling short of their expectations. You have probably heard that studies show most sales are lost due to communication failure. Personally, I think this simplifies why most sales are lost but this communication breakdown is why this book is so important.

Wouldn't it be cool if you could get into your clients' heads? Once you are aware of their visualizations, you won't make the mistake of focusing on YOUR visions by accident like I did in my previous Christmas Day Story.

> **" " Diagnostic Statements flush out your clients' visualizations thus reducing the risk of communication misinterpretations, disappointments, disconnects, or breakdowns.**

Too many times, the client's expectations do not match the sales person's interpretations of those expectations.

These communication challenges often result in unnecessary lost sales. But this can be avoided with some simple changes to the way in which we communicate.

I have conducted this exercise hundreds of times since 2007. Most people say they see physical items such as bags of money, coins, stacks of currency, and bags of gold. Others see symbols like a $ dollar, € Eur o, ¥ Yen, or £ Pound. Some of the more creative and humorous responses I have heard are things like the alimony check I write each month, my mortgage payment, bills, my tuition payment, my home, my children, my spouse, my parents...the list goes on and on.

I invited people on LinkedIn to participate in this exercise; with the promised they would be included in this book. Here are some of those responses:

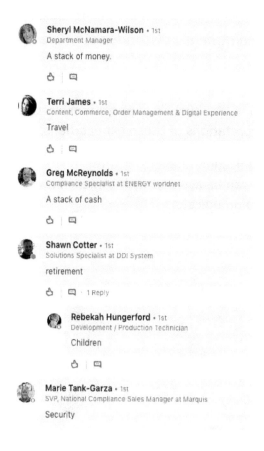

The main lesson learned in Exercise #1 may shock many readers but **there are no right or wrong answers when asked to describe what is visualized when hearing the word *MONEY*. This exercise demonstrated that each person will TRANSLATE or convert those letters into something meaningful that is unique to him or her.**

Therefore, this exercise proves that presenting WHAT your company does and WHY it does it, is NOT effective and is high risk. It is up to the sales person to convert and translate those features and functions into something that the client can relate, comprehend, understand, and VISUALIZE. You will be surprised as your clients describe how they will benefit from your products and/or services. You will witness the power of them selling themselves.

❝❝The biggest surprise in this exercise is not what people say in response. It is what they DON'T say that should make every single reader change the way in which he or she communicates.

Here is the part of Exercise #1 that should make those light bulbs start going off for many readers:

No matter what answers I have heard through the years, from all these hundreds of exercises, not one person has ever said they saw a slide with a bullet and the LETTERS – M.O.N.E.Y.

We simply do not visualize letters or words. In fact, our brains are a lot like a computer. Computers convert 1's and 0's to something on the screen that we can comprehend. Our brains do the same thing when they convert letters to physical things that we comprehend. So my question to each reader is:

❝❝WHY DO WE KEEP PRESENTING SLIDES LOADED WITH BULLETS AND LETTERS?

Why are most business books full of words yet very few pictures?

Why create any marketing materials loaded with pictures that have zero to do with the topic?

Your presentations MUST have visuals and these visuals must tie back to your message.

Your message should be delivered as a story that helps ensure your client can Relate, Retain, and Repeat.

❝❝ These are the Three R's of Visualization Diagnostic Statements

Relate - Retain - Repeat

With the "Three R's" in mind, let's stop for a moment and reflect on the first story in this book. Remember the roast story with the mother and daughter? As you read this, what did you visualize? Do you see the drawings or do you see the letters? I ask you again, "Why do our marketing materials, slides, brochures, websites, and infographics have so many words?" Why do we prefer to watch videos on YouTube instead of reading how to do something? The answer is that we want that visual translation done for us. We don't want our brains to do that work. We are only human. And guess what? The last time I checked, our clients are human too.

The most common mistake I see sales and companies make is to list out all their features and functions with the expectation that the clients will accurately TRANSLATE those details into how it applies to their own world. Depending upon clients to make that translation is a huge mistake. It is extremely risky to assume your clients WANT to convert your presentation or if they even know how!

As you can imagine, I have been talking about these principles to many people with various careers. I had a realtor friend of mine say that this doesn't apply to their business because clients buy homes based upon number of bedrooms and bathrooms. I thought that was an interesting perspective. The best realtor I ever met told me that she didn't sell homes she sold dreams. She sold us two homes and not once did we discuss number of bedrooms or bathrooms. Instead, she asked me to describe how I envisioned living in my next home.

I explained that our friends lost all of their children in a fire because all the kids were upstairs and the master was downstairs. I told her I would like the downstairs to have a nice flow for entertaining but that I preferred all the bedrooms be located upstairs. I described wanting to wake up in the mornings and step out on the balcony that overlooked a pool. I wanted fireplaces downstairs but I thought a fireplace in the master bedroom was romantic. I told her that I didn't care about the kitchen because I prefer to eat out but that I wanted a breakfast area to drink coffee and look at the pool. I explained that my husband and I both needed offices away from each other. I told her that I loved the look of a spiraling staircase but that wasn't mandatory. As I described these things to her, I felt emotional and anxious while I wondered if my perfect dream home even existed.

Well, it did exist. It was the first and only house she showed us and it was nothing like we imagined. It was a Georgian Style and that wasn't something we thought we wanted. When we pulled up, my husband didn't even want to go inside. But the realtor talked us into taking a look because she said she thought we would be surprised. As we walked through the house, my husband was unimpressed with the colors and the style. But I realized she was showing me my exact description! She did a great job bringing my thoughts to the surface so as I walked through the house, those thoughts were already on my mind and I was able to help my husband see the potential. I instantly imagined how we would live in the house. I never even noticed how many bedrooms. For the record, it had five but two of them became offices. We bought this house in 2000 and have lived in our dream home ever since. Do you realize all the time and inconvenience this realtor managed to avoid for all concerned? She was brilliant for asking me to describe how I wanted to live in the house instead of asking how many bedrooms or bathrooms we wanted. This quick sell gave her more time to show more homes to more people. If we ever sell, she will be the first one I call because I know there won't be a lot of unnecessary strangers in our home.

I see realtor ads all the time that describe the number of bedrooms and the number of baths along with a picture of a home. If we had seen an elevation of our current home with a description of five bedrooms and four bathrooms, we would have never agreed to look at it. So do ads that start off with number of bedrooms and bathrooms really do an effective job attracting the right buyers to the right homes?

Our realtor did us a great service by asking how we envisioned living in the home versus asking us what features and functions we THOUGHT we wanted. By doing this, she triggered emotions that I didn't even know I had! She was using neuroscience before I even knew what it was!

The Power of Translation

Exercise #1 demonstrated the power of visualization and why it is critical yet extremely complicated and difficult. Since we know words mean different things to different people, sales must take accountability for ensuring accurate and effective **translations.** Sales must convert the marketing message and guide the client's vision toward real life execution. How do you know that the way your offerings were designed is the best way for your clients to leverage them?

An Accidental Client Translation Success Story

Earlier, I described losing a sale due to a translation error regarding working during Christmas. Now I want to share a story how I accidentally won a sale. Thanks to a very smart client, she was able to translate my marketing message into how she would actually USE my offering.

My company sold a small amount of software to a client in hopes that the quantities of the software license would grow after they saw the value. However, nobody was using it, so I insisted on conducting an on-site training session. We were teaching them how to use the software to restore their backups. Each student had his or her own monitor with the software running. We were in the middle of a hands on demonstration when suddenly, a woman shrieked with delight. She screamed, "You are teaching this all wrong! This is not a recovery tool, this is an application management tool and we have been looking for something like this for almost a year! " She then explained that they were about to lose a major government contract because an important application kept crashing their system and nobody could figure out what was causing it. All the vendors pointed fingers at each other. She called me over to her monitor and showed me that a hidden part of these applications was being misidentified by their virus detection system and destroyed. Now that they could see hidden files associated with all their applications, they could identify what was causing the crash and they would save their government contract. This resulted in one of the fastest closes of my career and to this day, is also the largest commission check I have ever earned... accidentally. The reality is that my client is the one that earned this commission! That's extremely difficult to admit.

❝❝ My COMPANY taught me to sell the way the product was designed to work.

❝❝ My CLIENT taught me how they could actually benefit from the software!

This was a huge lesson learned as these Visualization Diagnostic Statements evolved.

I was fortunate that I had a client in that classroom that was able to translate our marketing message into something meaningful to her company. Unfortunately this is extremely rare! We cannot rely on clients to do the translating. It is sales responsibility to do the work for the client.

I was conducting a workshop last week and I was told about an $80 million client that was lost to a competitor last year. The client's decision to make the change was because the competitor identified something they could do that was perceived as unattainable with the current provider. The sad part of this story is that the incumbent vendor COULD do the same service but the client was unable to translate the features and functions adequately. This was a very costly translation error that we all want to avoid.

When was the last time you reached out to your clients to understand how they use your offerings?

❝❝ Clients should be your primary source for the Client-centric results that are the main part of your diagnostic statements.

If you haven't read your case studies, you should start collecting the content right away. You will use this information when we begin creating your first statements. If you don't have case studies or something that describes success stories of clients, this may actually be a red flag with your current employer. Sadly, I have worked for companies that couldn't provide this information because the offerings were not real. I've also worked for other companies that didn't document client successes because they feared the information would get into the competitors hands. This is ridiculous but it is a fear that actually exists. Don't rely on marketing or your company to find these golden nuggets. You should be in front of existing clients anyway. Just as my client taught me a new way to sell my software, you may be surprised how much positive information you can learn from your existing clients. And if they are happy with your company and the results they are experiencing, they should be more than happy to share detailed results with you. They may even be willing to speak with other prospective clients as a reference for your company.

Exercise #2 will help you understand why translating must be the responsibility of the sales organization.

EXERCISE #2A and #2B
The Power of Translation

❝❝ Think about how many things you ask from your clients. Never expect them to think too much or do too much work. It is up to you to make every process easy and to do as much of the work yourself.

#2A - Read this slide. Can you do it? Do you have any slides like this one in your current presentation? If so, WHY?

The I'm Going To Overload You With Data Slide

- I plan to give you this deck so I want you to know every single word that I am going to say to you because I don't trust you to take good notes.
- I am sure you will be grateful for this deck full of words and bullets so you don't have to take notes anyway.
- In addition, I can't recall exactly what I need to say to you so my slides are actually my script which will ensure I tell you every single thing I want you to know.
- My first dozen slides will explain to you how awesome my company is and why we are better than the competition. Which frankly, I am shocked you didn't already do this research before inviting me in to speak with you.
- I am also going to tell you all the industry issues that you already know, which will make you think I am super credible and you will want to buy from me.
- I am also going to provide donuts and lunch, despite the fact that you probably only eat Gluton Free or Keto foods. Because I was taught to build a relationship and that if I bring comfort food, you will like me and we will have a relationship and we all know that people buy from people that they like so this is yet another reason you will want to buy from me.
- It really doesn't even matter to me if you need or want to know all these things because if I use a projector to throw everything up on a wall, I will then be able to ask you to pick and choose all the services and/or products you will want to purchase.
- Our legal team made me promise to include a bullet with legal jargon indemnifying them from liability if and when I say something to you that may not be true. Furthermore, by reading this, you must release my company from any liability because what I say to you today is not necessarily endorsed by my company.
- What I am selling you today will make you so happy. You will increase your revenues, you will reduce your costs, you will automate and replace headcount (but don't tell your employees this one), and we are so much better than our competition because our stock prices are much higher due to our President's speeches each quarter that explain foreign currency fluctuations are the only reason our sales ever appear to be down.
- Oh and since I was just trained to be a consultative sales representative, I am also going to have slides full of questions that I need you to answer so that my management can see that I asked questions instead of just reading these slides to you during this presentation.
- After this meeting, I will schedule another meeting to get back to you so I can present to you everything you just told me. Even though I know you obviously already know it.

#2B – This is an original draft concept for the cover of this book. Read what this graphic says out loud.

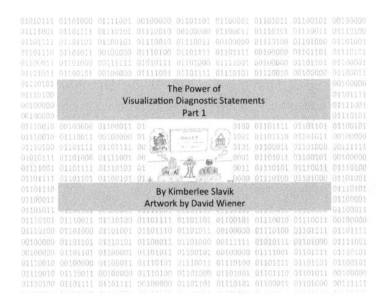

IMPORTANT - Stop and do that before reading any further.

In #2B, if you said that it says *" The Power of Visualization Diagnostic Statements Part 1, By Kimberlee Slavik, Artwork by David Wiener,"* you are only partially correct. Did you count the word, *Money* on the artwork? Do you realize that your brain took the easy route and read the letters that combined to make words and sentences? Did you take time to analyze the artwork or try and understand it? Most people do not take the time to do that either. You may have even taken an easier route and not read it at all!

Regardless of what exactly you read, not one person has taken the more challenging route and converted the 0s and 1s to words. If you actually did this, I want to meet you! If you didn't think to translate these binary numbers to letters, this is your next exercise. Convert this into words –

```
01010111 01101000 01111001 00100000
01101101 01100001 01101011 01100101
00100000 01111001 01101111 01110101
01110010 00100000 01100011 01110101
01110011 01110100 01101111 01101101
01100101 01110010 01110011 00100000
01110100 01101000 01101001 01101110
01101011 00100000 01110100 01101111
01101111 00100000 01101101 01110101
01100011 01101000 00111111
```

The background on the previous graphic is difficult to read. These are the actual numbers that ask an important question.

Do you know how to do this? If not, go to Appendix for a legend that will help you translate this. However, you will not find the translation anywhere in this book. So far, as of this first printing, not one person could tell me what this says.

Lessons Learned From Exercise #2

Despite the instructions above and multiple reiterations of why readers should do these exercises, over 90% of you will refuse to translate #2B and about the same percent will refuse to read the slide in #2A. Almost everybody will ignore the instructions. Why? Could it be because it is too much work? **Too many words or too many charts will have the same impact on your clients.**

Think about this – you have decided to read this book in order to improve something in your life. However, most of you are not willing to put in the effort required to maximize your results.

Isn't that the same logic we have for our clients? They are looking to make the best decision, so why do they also ignore important, bullet filled, generic claims in your presentation?

Why would you expect a different behavior from your clients than you see from your own self? What could have been done differently to get you more eager to participate? You will learn the changes that need to take place to engage your clients and improve the effectiveness of your value proposition and value. *The easier you make it for your audience, the more engaged they will become!*

? For those that didn't do either exercises in #2, your flight instinct kicked in.
Does that surprise you?
Are you doing the same thing to your clients?
Could this be how your competitors beat you?

Why wouldn't you expect the same avoidance from a client that you just dumped a folder full of documents such as a presentation, a long email, a bunch of URLs, a brochure, acronyms, industry jargon, or some other sort of marketing collateral that you sincerely thought would trigger buying behaviors? Why do we have slides that have pretty backgrounds versus backgrounds that help the audience retain the content? Why are we surprised when we don't get a response? Do you send emails hoping to get meetings? Do YOU read your SPAM or junk mail? Is selling to you via email effective? If not, why are you doing the same things to your clients? Does it feel good to tell yourself that you made some sort of effort? Marketing teams get excited when they see a 3%-5% response from marketing campaigns. Why is that acceptable? What if we could improve those percentages by doing things differently?

❝ Diagnostic Statements will increase your success significantly because they avoid triggering this avoidance response.

For the <10% of you that actually did translate the binary numbers, was this translation painful? Just as computers convert 0s and 1s into letters for us to understand, words in a brochure or slide must be converted by our clients for them to envision how the words relate to their lives.

! **As a READER, you are attempting to translate**
what you are reading right now
into ways you will use this.
As a WRITER, I am trying to translate for you!
It's not easy or everybody would be doing it!

This conversion is necessary for true comprehension. Yet, how many clients make the time to go through this process? I suspect that the numbers are very low. When we load decks up with bullets and words, we force our clients to translate those words and letters into something meaningful in their lives. Guess what? The chances of that happening are about the same percentages of those that followed instructions in Exercise #2.

Many readers will go to Appendix looking for the translated answer, which is why you won't find it. What is stronger in you; your flight instinct or curiosity? Chances are that your flight is stronger. So why expect a different response from your clients?

To those of you that actually read the slide as instructed in 2A, was it also painful? What did you have to do to read it? Did you have to blow it up? Most people will move on before they are forced to make an extra effort. How many points in the bullets can you recall or recite? The more you have to work, the less you will comprehend and retain.

Most of the bullets are satiric in nature and make fun of slides that are common and probably in your current presentations. Ironically, those that did put in the extra effort and read the slide actually reported back that the content was funny and made them realize how silly several of their current slides were from their clients' perspectives.

Both parts of this exercise made you work too hard and your "flight" instinct was activated.

Why are you doing this to your clients with your brochures and pre-sentations?

"" Diagnostic Statements eliminate this translation step, which is why your clients will engage and comprehend much faster.

EXERCISE #3- Creating your first Diagnostics Statements

This exercise will get you prepared for Chapter Two. This is a Treo Cell Phone. It was one of the first smart devices for sale yet the company is no longer in business. This picture represents how they sold their phone. Keep in mind, this was during a time when most people still had separate devices for storing client contact information, cameras, and calendars, just to name a few. Over fifteen years ago, cell phones were only used to make calls and do some very primitive texting.

If you saw an advertisement with these features and functions listed, how would you translate this data? How would this fancy phone make your life better? You have a huge advantage over the original consumers reading this advertisement because you can relate to it already. But imagine if you had never seen a cell phone do anything beyond making a call! Imagine when texting meant you had to push the #2 key three times to type a letter C!

Imagine it is 2002 and you saw this ad. Translate and convert at least EIGHT of these features into how you would use it. How could this phone make your life better? What would you be able to do differently with this smart device that you couldn't do with a typical cell phone? Unlike the previous 'lessons learned' summaries after each exercise, Chapter Two will unveil the importance of this exercise.

1.
2.
3.
4.
5.
6.
7.
8.

CHAPTER TWO

The Conversion Process

Conversion is a form of translation. Converting features and functions into Visualization Diagnostic Statements is the act of translating vendor centric wording into a description that the client can relate.

Because this chapter is extremely important, let me elaborate on the significance of Exercise #3.

Observations During the Birth of Smart Devices

This is the a story about the demise of one of the first smart phones and why identifying vendor content from client content is critical to creating successful Visnostic Statements.

Blackberry and Treo were two of the first Smart Phones released. I saw my first Treo advertisement in Fortune Magazine right after travel was horribly impacted by the tragedy of 911. The ad made such an impact on me, that I pulled the page out of my magazine and immediately contacted Sprint to get details about changing service providers. Despite having one of the best service contracts at the time, I was willing and eager to change carriers just to get this phone into my life. The ad mentioned the only carrier that would offer this phone would be Sprint. So the ad was effective. Right? Actually, it was not. I was one of a small minority that looked at this ad and TRANSLATED it into why I cared.

The airports were miserable immediately after the attacks on 9/11. Internet existed but it wasn't widely available and it was expensive. The ad I saw was very similar to this photo.

Here are some actual results from that translation and what my responses would have been in Exercise #3:

1. The ad said I could send and receive email without Internet. I translated this to mean that I could do email at the airport for the first time ever from a PHONE! I could actually be productive while waiting for delayed flights to arrive.

2. It said it had a keyboard. This meant I would no longer need to hit the #2 key three times in order to type a C!

3. It said it had a camera. This meant I didn't need to lug around my camera, charger, and accessories anymore.

4. It said I could store my client phone numbers on my phone. PalmPilot made Treo and it was one of the first phones that actually stored contacts' phone numbers in the phone. This meant that I could transfer all of my contacts from the PalmPilot I carried everywhere into my phone and not have to carry yet another device or its charger around airports anymore.

5. It showed some of the apps that were included. I noticed that there was a calendar app, which meant I could throw away my bulky and heavy day timer.

6. It said that the phone had a stylus. I admit this one stumped me. I had to do some research to figure out why I should care about this. I uncovered that another app was for taking notes and I could use a stylus to write on the screen just like I would in a journal. This was another excuse to ditch the heavy and bulky day timer and pen.

You get the picture. How did your translation in Exercise #3 compare to mine? I imagine it would be different since Smart Phones are now an integral part of our culture. The point of all this is that Treo stressed the components, features, and functions of it's wonderful device. They hoped that consumers were smart enough to translate that into how it would make their lives better. I was able to do that, but they really missed out on a huge opportunity to gain and keep a much larger market share. Back in those days, a phone was a phone. Period. The concept of a device that was basically a miniature computer was really difficult for most of society to comprehend. Those of us in the technology world had an easier time understanding the vision and potential of these types of devices. However, we were a minority from the general population. Blackberry was basically marketing the same way so the consumers that DID figure out the translation then had to choose between two phones that sounded almost exactly the same.

Then came Apple's iPhone and things changed RAPIDLY. Do you recall the original iPhone commercials? They never talked about the storage, the operating system, the applications, or any technical specs at all. They showed cool people doing cool things like listening to music, taking pictures and video, and having a great time! They showed how this new device was going to change lives for the better and people would have fun while doing it! Again, those commercials told a story; it didn't put us into a coma with all the features and functions or speeds and feeds and it worked so well that Treo no longer exists and Blackberry continues to struggle for market share. In contrast,

Apple is worth billions of dollars and almost every person reading right now has had at least one iPhone. This is such a great example of what happens when you create Vendor-centric messaging versus client-centric messaging in your marketing content.

Thanks to Apple's translation efforts, the majority of the population finally understood how these incredible Smart Devices could change lives for the better. Apple figured out a way to paint the vision for the clients and help them avoid that translation requirement. Treo and Blackberry were completely blindsided by Apple's unique marketing approach as Apple took market share (in what felt like) overnight.

What Great Salespeople Do taught us that decisions are made with the emotional side of our brain, not the logical side. Which side do you think is stimulated with technical details? If people make emotional buying decisions, why do we include technical details? Apple has done a brilliant job making us emotional about our Apple products.

The Temptation to Kill Our Clients With Data

Because of the rise and fall I observed of these two incredibly innovative companies, I became very analytical of the presentation materials of companies that I represented.

I believe that the inability to articulate a message that resonated with the general public, and the marketing of features and functions, are what led to the eventual demise of Treo.

Therefore, when I start with a new company, one of the first things I want to see is the corporate sales presentation. I was with a Fortune 500 company that was ranked in the top 50. Surprisingly, their deck was over 180 slides of technical details! I asked my coworkers if they really subjected their client base to this deck and they confirmed that not only was accurate, it took a full day to go through the entire deck! I also want to mention that sales were in a decline and all the competitors were picking off loyal, long-term clients at an alarming rate. Any guesses why?

After several years of reviewing feature and function marketing collateral and translating them so I could create my own sales tools, I have finally created a formalized process that I conduct today as full day translation workshop.

NOTE: During the feedback collected when this book was a draft, several reviewers pointed out that their respective industries did not use many presentations. What you are about to read is an analysis of a Slide Deck used for presentations. However, these same principles apply to any marketing messaging.

This analysis process applies to all forms of marketing, including website content, mobile device applications, brochures, infographics, or any other marketing tools you use to share your business with prospective clients.

Step 1 – Analyze Your Content – Transcribe & Categorize by Segmentation

For Step One, have someone give the presentation and record it. If they used a script, get an electronic copy of that, as well. It will help during the transcription and categorization process. Try and separate Vendor-centric components of the presentation from the client-centric content in the presentation. If your presentation is very feature/function or product focused, try and separate content from what you do and how the client will use it. Keep an eye out for buzz words, acronyms, and keep a list so you avoid them. The main things you want to pull out for your Visnostic Statements are the client centric points. The most powerful things that all clients want to know are the results. Be sure and categorize all results. For example, reduction of costs, improve efficiencies, return on investment are typical declarations of results I have seen in almost every sales presentation.

After the content is separated into either vendor or client categories, I then create sub-categories under each main category. For example, I just recently evaluated a presentation and created the following breakdowns:

Sample Client-centric Subcategories –

Client challenges, complexity, results, outcome, miscellaneous content

Sample Vendor-centric Subcategories –

Vendor specific details such as jargon, acronyms, technical terminology, definitions, features and functions, and any other specific services or product details

The best way to properly learn the process is to have an actual presentation to dissect. Although I have access to many of the presentations of various employers, to avoid legal issues or any embarrassment to any of them, I will select a random slide deck to walk you through. I went to a website in which you may be familiar - https://www.slideshare.net. I did a simple search for "sales presentation" and flipped through several results from my query.

As I was sifting through the slide decks, the first thing I did was to look for a fortune 50 company to analyze. Then I went to check to see how many slides were in each deck. They ranged from 34 (the smallest deck I opened) to over 100 slides.

One of the cool things that I like about this site is that it will tell you on each slide the number of people that have "clipped" your slide. This often gives hints about which slides resonate the most. The problem is that you don't know with whom it is resonating. Is it someone stealing your data for their own decks, a client, a student, a competitor, or a coworker?

A clip notification also demonstrates which ones are NOT resonating as well. As you analyze your own deck, you may want to consider sharing it on a sight like this. Not only will you be able to determine which slides are your most intriguing, but it also informs you of the number of times the deck has been viewed, comments, thumbs up, and number of times it was downloaded.

If you are exploring other company's decks, you can determine how old the deck is by how long ago it was uploaded. You can also share this by sending it to someone or even to yourself for future reference.

As I flipped through multiple decks, I couldn't help notice that most of the statements in the decks are so generic in nature that it is difficult to determine what is being sold. These decks could be recycled and could be used to sell anything from software to home appliances.

They all articulate that what you are selling will save money. They claim they are more efficient than the competitors or the incumbent provider. They brag about the ease of use while describing why their offering is better than the competitors. They basically describe how their offering will catapult their clients into Nirvana. But per our knowledge of Neuroscience, this approach misses the mark because these decks rarely answer WHY, HOW, or WHAT and more importantly, most decks do not nurture a dialogue or two-way communication. And the slides that do have visual aids often use charts and graphs. And while they can tell a pretty impressive story, some are so complex, that they make the brain work way too hard to translate the meaning in order to decipher the story from them.

The reality is that most decks are created by individuals that are well trained to know what the current "in" colors are, the coolest fonts to use, what graphics can be used legally, the card stock on which to print them, and other cosmetically appealing details (marketing) OR they are created by those that understand HOW the product works (techies). **But very rarely have these deck creators ever purchased what they are trying to help the sales organization sell.**

I apologize to anybody that currently has ruffled feathers but please bear with me. I want this knowledge to make its way into marketing departments all over the world, so I am writing this with the hopes that clients, sales people, leaders, and marketing people all benefit from these words. **I am not saying that your baby is ugly. I want to help you make your baby more beautiful, interesting, and effective.**

Remember the first story I told in the Preface about the family roast recipe? Do you recall that the moral to the story was that we should do things differently? *The Challenger Sale* encourages doing things differently versus being status quo and this approach is very different. More importantly, it's already been proven that it works.

How many readers will admit that the first thing you do when you are about to get a presentation, is look in the bottom left hand corner of the screen to see how many slides you will have to endure?

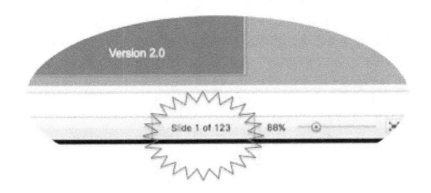

Yikes! **123 slides?** Flight instinct engaged!

Do you recall when you were in school and you walked into class and saw a projector or television, you were excited because you knew you were about to see a film versus enduring a lecture? Humans want visuals. We want to be entertained. We love stories. Presentations used to be super cool when the technology was new. Today, it is torture, not because presentations are outdated but because too many people don't know how to create them the way our brains want them to be delivered. I am about to show you how to ditch the words to make your message less painful AND be remembered AND get your audience emotionally engaged! I am also going to show you a way to give this presentation without Internet, over lunch, on a golf course, or any other place that won't be technology friendly.

After sifting through dozens of decks, I found a presentation with thirty-two slides from a Fortune Ten company. They spent the first 12 slides explaining to the clients why doing it their current way was wrong. They also used those slides to brag about their own company's competencies and awards. How many readers have this same formatted deck? *The Challenger Sale* teaches that most clients don't invite salespeople back for the second meeting because we didn't tell them anything they didn't already know. In other words, we didn't provide value during the first meeting! It wasn't until slide 13 that the deck started articulating what the client wanted to hear, which described the unique benefits of doing business with this Fortune Ten company. However, if the attention span really is only eight minutes, the audience has already disengaged. As I read through their points, I wondered if they even asked their audience WHAT was important to THEM before they made assumptions. By slide 15, the deck started getting into some technical features and functions.

While I was analyzing this online deck it wasn't until slide 18 that they started getting into the generic ways their software made life better. Why waste time with 17 slides the client wasn't there to learn? By slide 18 the client was already thinking about what they were going to have for dinner! I am not being sarcastic. Remember my previous story when my client was writing feverously? I walked over to him to see his notes and it was his grocery list? My deck had this exact format! I know that if I were a buyer, I would do my research on a company before I invited them to my site to take up my valuable time. So do you really need those first slides? Are they worth the risk of losing your audience's attention? Ask yourself, if you only had eight minutes with your prospective client, which points would be the most important points to THEM?

Slides 19, 22, 25, and 28 were placeholders that were each titled "Demo" so the client actually got to see this offering in action. This made my analysis a bit challenged because there is nothing in the deck describing what they were going to be shown. The header in Slide 30 said, "Now, what are you waiting for?" I assume this was their attempt to flush out a sense of urgency in the client.

Overall, I would have given this deck a "D" grade. The final slide was a bio on the speaker. She appears to be a technology expert versus a sales professional or marketing expert. I wish there was a way to know what percentage of her presentations proceeded through the sales cycle. I suspect the number is very low. But in all fairness, I looked at other decks as well. I chose this one as an example because it is a Fortune 10 company and had the least number of slides.

All of the decks I reviewed seemed to follow the same pattern: build credibility, talk about industry pains, and then data dump all the specs about the offering. Most decks could really be done with one to three slides if we were to keep in mind what the audience truly wants. What if I told you that you could be more impactful with ZERO slides? That is the direction in which we are heading. You will learn more about this in Chapter Four.

For Step One of your own analysis, you should have been able to eliminate most of the slides. Only keep the ones that articulate results or differentiators to the clients. Leave out anything pertaining to your company, the stock price, etc. Keep asking yourself, "WHY would a potential client care about this slide?" As you go through your deck, note all the points that reference results. You will use these to convert your slides into your Visnostic Statements later.

Step 2 – Gather Your Case Studies or References

Our minds want stories and what better stories than those from our most successful and happy clients? Case Studies are typically full of the results we are looking for, but very few clients have legal teams that will allow them to be actual references due to fears of lawsuits from competitors. Clients love to help you and can give you valuable perspective from their point of view. Plus, you may gather additional off the record comments that got cut by legal when the case studies and results were originally constructed. Be sure and keep names out of your Visnostic Statements. Instead, memorize the details because this process tends to be interactive. Your potential clients will enjoy these stories of success as you walk through each Diagnostic Statement. Keep a look out for results and timelines.

Step 3 – Creating the Visnostic Statements

By now, you have narrowed down the content in your presentation to only the details that will challenge your client to do things differently and you now have case studies. And the client centric content should now stand out with your highlights or notes.

Because this is the most important step, I have devoted an entire chapter to converting your presentation data into Visnostic Statements. Chapter Three will go into greater detail with how to create powerful Visnostic Statements.

A major point worth mentioning now is that if you struggle creating these statements, this is a huge red flag. You will need to figure out if the problem is the current marketing content, poor training, lack of client success stories, or weak sales skills. Those that know the results of their offering will find the creation of VDS to be easy and fun to do. Those that don't understand your offering will struggle. Workshops can help if this is difficult.

Step 4 – Have Your Visnostic Statements Verified Internally

I recommend before you approach a client with the Visnostic Statements you converted, that you verify the accuracy of each statement internally. Also, run these by your manager and/or someone in marketing to ensure you have interpreted and con-verted the presentation and case study content accurately. The last thing you want to happen is that you misrepresent your com-pany's capabilities or results. Great sales professionals do not lie or misrepresent their offerings.

Step 5 – Format the Columns Into a Spreadsheet versus a Document

I have mentioned multiple times that this process has evolved and one of these improvements is the formatting in a spreadsheet ver-sus a document. Spreadsheets allow formulas to be written that will aid in the translation process and generate the client deliverable. I recommend that you work with your IT department to create for-mulas to calculate the responses by the client. Because what was developed at previous companies is the property of those compa-nies, I commissioned someone I respect to help me create detailed instructions for my readers. This will be described in great detail in Chapter Five.

Step 6 – Name Your New Tool

I have called these discussion tools by different names based upon the specific business I was representing. They have been called a "Pre-call Survey" when I used them to prep for a big meeting. I have also called the discussion process a "Health Check" and a "Free Assessment." I have even customized the name at various shows, events, and conferences to reflect the event name. For our purpose, I will refer to the tool as a Diagnostics Tool.

Step 7 – Proto Type Your New Tool with Current Clients

My favorite way to work out the bugs and revise this is to take a client that I have a wonderful relationship with to lunch. I basically recreate the story I told you earlier by asking the client to do me a favor by going through this process. In fact, I highly recommend doing this with as many existing clients as possible. This tool may seem like it is just for new clients, but you may be shocked how little your existing clients really know about your entire offering. This tool is a great conversation guide that will help you upsell your existing clients while strengthening your relationship. As I walked through the most recent tool I created, I realized it was way too long. I needed to get it down to the top ten statements. It actually took about six trial runs to identify the top ten that created the most emotions and interest. Most of these were universally appealing but there were a few that excited some of my clients and not others. So I actually ended up with a top 15, which was a huge reduction from 30 original statements. I ended up keeping all the statements but "hid" them in my spreadsheet in case I needed them in the future. I also hoped that I would find a client that would appreciate a deeper dive into their assessment so keeping all the statements hidden yet available is a great practice.

Step 8 – Decide on a venue for delivering your Diagnostic Statements.

A venue can be a location and it can also be the way in which it is conducted; it could be a hard copy or an electronic version for a tablet. Each response can be saved on the table or on an application in the cloud. I use Survey Monkey as a cloud venue for assessing potential

DynaExec clients. This is what is posted on my website (www.dynaex-ec.com). https://www.surveymonkey.com/r/TR73SMS

After a potential client completes the statements, the responses are sent to a dedicated email address:

Assess Your Current Sales Management

1. DynaExec Assessment Survey

Most Sales VPs fail within 12 months. Take this brief survey to find out how your company would benefit from DynaExec.

1. We have full confidence in the sales and marketing management teams that are driving results.

○ We would LIKE to say this today but we currently can not do this.

○ We CAN SAY this today and we are satisfied.

○ We CAN SAY this today but it needs improvement.

○ This is not important, it's not applicable, or I don't know.

2. Our marketing team has done a brilliant job translating features and functions into language that our clients understand.

○ We would LIKE to say this today but we currently can not do this.

○ We CAN SAY this today and we are satisfied.

○ We CAN SAY this today but it needs improvement.

○ This is not important, it's not applicable, or I don't know.

3. Sales and revenues are satisfactory or exceeding expectations.

○ We would LIKE to say this today but we currently can not do this.

○ We CAN SAY this today and we are satisfied.

○ We CAN SAY this today but it needs improvement.

○ This is not important, it's not applicable, or I don't know.

4. The current management team has a successful track record driving results and revenues.

○ We would LIKE to say this today but we currently can not do this.

○ We CAN SAY this today and we are satisfied.

○ We CAN SAY this today but it needs improvement.

○ This is not important, it's not applicable, or I don't know.

5. A thorough market research has been performed and our company service or product is being marketed effectively.

◯ We would LIKE to say this today but we currently can not do this.

◯ We CAN SAY this today and we are satisfied.

◯ We CAN SAY this today but it needs improvement.

◯ This is not important, it's not applicable, or I don't know.

6. Our messaging incorporates neuroscience in all messaging.
Therefore, our sales have increased using Visualization Diagnostic Statements.

◯ We would LIKE to say this today but we currently can not do this.

◯ We CAN SAY this today and we are satisfied.

◯ We CAN SAY this today but it needs improvement.

◯ This is not important, it's not applicable, or I don't know.

7. The current management team is 100% honest during the business reviews and is at least 75% accurate with forecasting sales.

◯ We would LIKE to say this today but we currently can not do this.

◯ We CAN SAY this today and we are satisfied.

◯ We CAN SAY this today but it needs improvement.

◯ This is not important, it's not applicable, or I don't know.

8. The proper Lead Generation efforts are being made. The pipeline is healthy and growing with solid business leads and opportunities.

◯ We would LIKE to say this today but we currently can not do this.

◯ We CAN SAY this today and we are satisfied.

◯ We CAN SAY this today but it needs improvement.

◯ This is not important, it's not applicable, or I don't know.

9. Our current clients are very happy and eager to be references. We leverage their success to build our business.

◯ We would LIKE to say this today but we currently can not do this.

◯ We CAN SAY this today and we are satisfied.

◯ We CAN SAY this today but it needs improvement.

◯ This is not important, it's not applicable, or I don't know.

* 10. Find out your results!

Provide your contact information such as your name, title, company, email address, and phone number and we will respond promptly with a FREE Assessment and recommendation!

Thank you for taking the FREE Sales and Leadership Assessment Survey sponsored by DynaExec! www.dynaexec.com

```
┌─────────────────────────────┐
│                             │
│                             │
│                             │
└─────────────────────────────┘
```

```
┌──────────┐
│   Done   │
└──────────┘
```

Step 9 – Arrange a Workshop and Consulting.

This step is optional but will expedite this process and get deliverables in sales hands much more efficiently. However, my objective is to describe how to do this with so much detail, that you can do this without a workshop.

The first workshop was conducted before this book was even published and it was a huge success. Thankfully, the client agreed to allow me to share the format that was created during the workshop. It includes the 1-5 scoring system that was developed several years ago. It also includes the fairly new Segments column to help identify and organize the Visnostic Statements by vendor business or product areas.

Some examples of potential segment names include financial impact, hardware, software, consulting, and specific products and services. This Segment column is very important because it will enable users to quickly identify and organize the strengths, weaknesses, and moderate areas of your clients' current abilities.

Furthermore, segments will aid in pin pointing the areas to prioritize sales efforts. Segments can also reverse our translation back to which products or services sales will focus future efforts.

In Chapter Two, you have learned about how to start gathering the data needed to create the Visnostic Statements in your new Diagnostics Tool. But as I mentioned previously, having people respond to your Diagnostic Statement is basically gathering data. We must convert that data into valuable information.

Chapter Three will dive deep into creating your statements, Chapter Four will help you understand the importance of graphics, and Chapter Five will cover how to convert that data into something your client will value and be proud to circulate internally on your behalf.

CHAPTER THREE

Creating Impactful Visualization Diagnostic Statements

How to Convert Bullets to EFFECTIVE "Visnostic Statements"

There are two components to converting marketing messages into a Visnostic Statement approach. You will need the actual Visnostic Statements and then you will need to create appropriate responses. I know I am repeating myself but repetition equates to retention so always do your responses in threes so they are multiple choice and never allow the responses to be close-ended with a yes or no response. Close-ended questions will not engage the emotions you need from your participant.

Ensure the statements are positive.

Before I got married, I got some incredible advice from a counselor about raising children. The counselor described a scenario to me that took place in a packed grocery store and my future child was throwing a fit and embarrassing me. The scenario went on that my first instinct in that moment will be to tell the child that if he or she behaved, we could go get a new toy or get some ice cream after we are done grocery shopping. The counselor continued by saying that this tactic will probably work – in the short term. He said that if I take this approach in teaching my child, I would be reinforcing bad behavior by rewarding them for acting out. In other words, I just taught my child that if he or she misbehaves or embarrasses me, they would be rewarded. The counselor then told me that this same rule applies to my marriage and to my working relationships with managers, clients, and coworkers. Never back down, ignore, or concede to someone that is behaving in a manner that is unacceptable because you are reinforcing bad behavior. So what does this have to do with creating effective Visnostic Statements? Here are two examples of statements that say the same thing. Can you **FEEL** the difference?

- I no longer dread Quarterly Reviews because our sales numbers have increased 10% each quarter.

- I enjoy Quarterly Reviews because our sales numbers have increased 10% each quarter.

Engaging the brain in positive visualization is a powerful approach. You read all the time about positive thinking and the power of positive thoughts. Therefore, it is imperative that when creating Visnostic Statements, that you are guiding the thought process towards positive energy, visions, and thoughts.

Despite doing these statements for over a decade, I just recently became aware of how important this advice really is. In fact, this past year I created a slide with a header that said something like, *Challenges Typical Clients Experienced BEFORE Becoming Clients.* There was a list of about a dozen scenarios describing how horrible things used to be. As this list was socialized internally, the content was not well received. By changing these "before" scenarios into "after" scenarios and rephrasing them into the client-centric language of Visnostic

Statements, the responses became much more enthusiastic, not just internally, but with potential clients as well. People truly want you to paint positive visualizations versus negative thoughts and images.

Include Results when possible.

Because I hire sales people, I have read hundreds of resumés. Surprisingly, most sales resumés are terrible. They ramble on about their territory, quotas, education, skills, etc. A hiring manager is very much a "Buyer;" and as a hiring manager, I want to read about results. Ok, so you had TOLA (Texas, Oklahoma, Louisiana, and Arkansas). I want to know how much you increased the pipeline and how fast you did it. While I like to know your quota, I really want to know how much you exceeded your quota. I am happy you had sales training, but how did you apply what you learned to become more successful? I would say that less than 10% of the resumés I've reviewed compelled me to want a discussion. Selling is exactly like interviewing. The client wants you to cut to the chase. What can you do and how fast can you do it to help them exceed their numbers?

Be careful that they are statements and not questions.

Do you recall when Strategic Selling and Consultative Selling were the desired approaches? I sold during those days and for the record, I am a huge believer in both the strategic and consultative sales THOUGHT PROCESSES. However, the approach around execution was extremely painful for the client and I avoid it at all costs. Often, it felt like some sort of competitive scenario with the client.

During my attempts at questioning clients, I noticed that the flaw in the consultative approach was that we almost became drill sergeants with our inquisitions. People do not like to be talked AT. Therefore it should be no surprise that they don't like to be in the hot seat with a barrage of questions either. Asking questions is an extremely cerebral activity and can trigger the wrong emotions by putting the client on the defense. Furthermore, filling out a questionnaire can be exhausting for all concerned and almost feel like an arm wrestling scenario.

Thankfully, this can be fixed very simply. The process will be so much more pleasant, for all concerned, by converting those questions into Visnostic Statements and having a more emotional versus cerebral conversation with the client.

Here is an example. Which of these sentences sound more compelling?:

Do you consider training to be a cost or investment?
(Question)

Or

Our current training program has made us an additional 28% profit each quarter and is no longer viewed as a cost center.
(Diagnostic Statement)

The magic of these statements versus questions is the way in which the brain has to process the data in order to respond. To trigger the positive chemical reactions, you must gather the data without blasting the client with questions. Remember, you are there to help them not to make them miserable.

The statement must be written as though the client is saying it, not you or your company.

Here are two statements. Which do you think will resonate with the client better?

- My company can save you one million dollars each quarter. (Vendor-centric)

- I save one million dollars each quarter. (Client-centric)

Avoid sounding generic.

A client also doesn't want to hear "We reduce costs…" "We save you money…" They hear this from every single vendor that walks in their door. They need and want you to be different. Let's start working on how we will help you be different.

Here is a typical bullet that most companies have in their presentation:

We save you money.

You probably have a bullet in your presentation right now that has something like this on it. Guess what? Your competitors do, too. This is so generic that you could be talking about retail items, outsourcing, technology items, natural resources, etc. Be more specific. Don't make your client think so much. Where are the results to back up this claim? I typically find these details in case studies or reference documents. Here is an actual Diagnostic Statement I re-wrote a few years ago:

I have reduced my costs by 23% in just six months after implementing similar software.

This wording answered the following questions:

How do you save money?

How much money do you save?

How fast do you save money?

Their response choices to these statements would be, "I can say this today." "I WISH I could say this today." Or "I don't know, it's not important, or not applicable."

❝❝ A Diagnostic Statement should contain facts, numbers, or statistics especially about quantities and timeframes.

A good source for these types of details can often be found in case studies. I have mentioned numerous times that our minds WANT stories. The best business stories of how your company has improved another client's business can be found in case studies.

To create a Diagnostic Statement, start with a result first to make the strongest emotional impact. A result could be an amount, timeframe, or both. By putting the results upfront, you immediately make a powerful emotional connection.

Then include how you did it. Try and map your feature/function slides to your case studies and you will have the ingredients for a powerful Diagnostic Statement! Often you will find that as you go through this process, the client will ask you questions or ask for more details. It is a wonderful way to start a discussion around other client successes so you better know your reference clients very well.

This method of communication where the client actually asks you for details is the best way to make the information resonate. If you just put a case study printout in a collateral package, it most likely won't be read; and, if it is read, there is the risk of distractions or lack of concentration by the client/reader. If they are asking you for details, they are engaged.

Let's do another one for practice. The more details in the Diagnostic Statement, the more mentally engaged your client would need to be in order to give an accurate response. However, be careful not to make the statements overly complicated or your client will get frustrated, confused, and annoyed. Here is another common claim by pretty much all companies:

We will improve your processes and make you more efficient.

This is Vendor-centric (We) and doesn't address what your client really wants to know. How much? How soon?

❝❝ Most content in a presentation speaks from your company's perspective (We) but a Diagnostics Statement speaks from your CLIENT's perspective (I).

How do you do it?

Convert that generic statement into something like this:

80% of the clients of my current vendor, report a decrease in human error by at least 90% and were able to reduce headcount by 20% due to automation.

This Diagnostics Statement is written as though the client said it. It describes results of automation, amounts, and timeframe. Again, their response choices would be, "I can say this today." "I WISH I could say this today." Or "I don't know, it's not important, or not applicable." And as mentioned earlier, not all client responses will be affirmations.

By now you should be seeing a tremendous improvement after converting words from your company's perspective to your client's perspective. They both make the same point but one is much more detailed and impactful. And more importantly, one is much more meaningful to the person that matters most – your prospective client!

The WAY it is stated, requiring a response, is significantly more engaging. Statements, when worded positively, force your clients' minds to envision themselves as a huge success using your products and/or services. **This is how you eliminate the translation process!**

In the past, when clients responded by telling me that they could do or say it today, I considered this response to mean that I didn't have an opportunity to sell them anything.

Today, if the client states "I can say this today," ask them to grade themselves 1-5, with 1 being "needs a lot of work" and 5 being "it can't get any better." When I originally made this revision several years ago, it was due to a suggestion from my CEO. I was shocked how many grades were 3 or less which meant that clients were open to a better way.

This new grading system really opened my eyes to how many current areas in which clients want to do better. So there really IS an opportunity for improvement here and it is an excellent way to get the client to give you even more details about any struggles or dissatisfactions they currently have. I highly recommend using this grading system right away and don't be bashful about asking them to elaborate on why they gave themselves a particular score. I have been shocked how much I learn with this simple follow-up question.

> **❝** Just because clients say they can do it today, doesn't mean they can't do it much better with your help!

I completely understand that this approach is not natural and can be difficult at first. If you need help, please send me your presentation and I will help you. Please use one of the emails I referenced. Once you get the hang of this methodology, the most difficult part will be to narrow down the Visnostic Statements to the best ten or less to make this process bearable for your client. I admit that this is my biggest weakness. I want to go through ALL the benefits because this becomes an incredible diagnostics tool to flush out all the ways in which I can help each potential client!

What a great problem to have!

EXERCISE #4 – Converting Features and Functions to Visnostic Statements

Here is an example conversion/translation exercise for you to do yourself. Leverage the details from the Case Study to convert the original presentation bullets into Visnostic Statements. The responses from your client to your newly created Diagnostics Statements should be "I WISH I could say this today! " "I CAN say this today." Or "I don't know, not important, or not applicable."

Case Study –

- XYZ Company became a client two years ago
- Spent $1 million in software and implementation
- Software took six months to implement

- Zero down time during conversion from old system to new one
- New system was more automated and reduced a headcount of $150k fully loaded personnel cost immediately after implementation
- Customer Satisfaction increases by 28% due to lack of human error
- Won two new customers worth over $12 million due to automation advantage over competition
- Closed these new clients in less than 10 months
- Return on Investment (ROI) was 12x cost

Original (VENDOR-CENTRIC) Presentation –

- We save money
- We provide a rapid ROI
- We increase revenues
- We improve customer service
- We help automate
- We reduce headcount
- We give our clients a competitive advantage in the marketplace
- Easy and fast implementation
- We are better than the competition
- No business disruption during implementation

Visnostic Statements (CUSTOMER-CENTRIC)
– Answers in Appendix

> I saved _____ per year within _____ months of purchasing new software.

> In under _____ of purchase, the ROI was _____ what I paid for it.

> Revenues increased by _____ in under _____ years due to increased client demand.

> Client satisfaction is at an all time high thanks to _____.

> _____ has given us a _____ advantage in the marketplace within _____ but more importantly; our new service is giving our clients a _____ as well.

> I am able to say we had an implementation that caused _____.

> I was promoted due to _____ _____.

> Write your own Diagnostic Statement.

While sample answers are located in Appendix, this doesn't mean that what you wrote was wrong. There really aren't right or wrong Visnostic Statements (unless they are inaccurate or ineffective). There ARE weaker or stronger statements. There ARE more impactful and more detailed statements. Some are impactful when they are simple. For example, I recently wrote one that stated "We have never been fined due to an employee being onsite and unqualified." This statement didn't have a timeframe or an amount but it definitely resonated. I was stunned how emotional the responses were to that one. It seemed that everybody said with passion that they WISHED they could say that today!

Practice them with your best clients. You will get better at this and you may be shocked how many things your existing clients either didn't know or they forgot. Don't be surprised if your first sales are from your existing clients! And you can close these sales during lunch or on a golf course! In addition to some easy and fast quota attainment, you will almost always get additional case study stories to incorporate into the next version of your Visnostic Statements.

Do you see the power behind changing a bullet that says "We save money" to "I saved $150k per year within six months of purchasing a new software." The second one answers how much was saved within what timeframe and how it was done. The details make it more impactful but having your client envision himself or herself saying it, is what triggers the brain to engage emotionally. This is exciting when you actually watch it work.

So to summarize what we learned in Chapter 3, you should now understand how to create powerful Visnostic Statements by combining results from case studies with your current marketing message. You can now start converting generic feature/function or speed and feed statements into powerful Visnostic Statements by combining the results with the function details.

CHAPTER FOUR

The Three R's of Visualization Diagnostic Statements
Retain, Relate, Repeat

Chapter Four is the shortest chapter, but it will help you gather your thoughts on the type of visuals you will want to include in your final deliverable to the client.

Most clients must not only understand the benefits of doing business with you, they must be able to remember your value proposition and articulate it internally. A great way for sales people to gauge how they are doing is to look for signs that your clients remember (RETAIN) your main points, comprehend (RELATE) them, and can share (REPEAT) your message internally when you are not available. Having impactful visualizations are key to ensuring your client can spread your message and become a very effective Champion for you and your company.

VISUALIZATIONS

VISUALIZATION AIDS MEMORY

Rw 2018

In just three chapters, you have learned why Visnostic Statements engage the emotions and thoughts of your clients. You now have learned how to take existing marketing messaging and case studies to create a Diagnostics discussion tool. Now that you have the information that you need from the client, we can start

79

to build your client deliverable. The deliverable that you give to the client must paint a vision of what could be versus giving your client a document full of what they just told you and they already know. So let's talk about why visuals will be an important element of the deliverable.

Basically, we have two ways in which to help others visualize our message. We can either paint a picture through our words and actions or we can literally paint a picture using graphics, photos, charts, or other forms of artwork. As sales professionals, we need to be able to do both.

Once you finish taking words from your brochures and presentations and convert them into Visnostic Statements, you are ready to create your deliverable. You have created a tool to gather data and diagnose your client's areas of weakness and strengths. However, data becomes valuable when it is converted into information. The final result will be a **memorable** deliverable for your client.

The Three R's – RETAIN – To Keep In One's Memory

The words retain and remember are interchangeable. I have found the best way to retain information is through visualizations and having impressive results in the content. So the first of the three R's actually includes the words retain, remember, and results.

Remembering names has always been one of my biggest challenges in business. When I was in my 20's, I took a continuing education course to help me with memorization. This class taught me to create "folders" in my brain for each name. So if someone told me that her name was Kristin, I should visualize a folder full of all the other Kristins I knew. I get it and it helped but I still stink at remembering names. I tried looking at names on badges but I can't recall names that way either. But I didn't give up on improving my memory.

I took another course a few weeks later that promised to help students remember presentations without index cards or notes and as a bonus, students would even learn how to make a grocery list without ever writing it down again.

This time, they taught us to envision our grocery items on parts of our body. We started at our feet. We were taught to imagine a carton of eggs on our feet, bananas stuck to our ankles, and a milk carton on our knee. You get the idea. I still do this today. And while it isn't perfect, it works pretty well.

As far as how to remember your presentation without note cards, the training advised going to the venue early and start at the left side of the room and envision your topics on the doors, windows, clocks, and other landmarks in the room. This also works fairly well. The audience thinks you are doing a great job scanning the people in the room and making eye contact with every person but you are actually focused on the items in the room like outlets or furniture. Again, it works great but it's not always perfect.

Why am I telling you these stories? Because it is 30 years later **and I still remember both of those presentations, the RESULTS from the education, and I retained the methodology I was taught.** Neither of the classes used presentations loaded with words. The only slides they showed us had pictures of what they instructed us to do. They stood in front of us and demonstrated how it worked and explained it to us and then the instructor had us work in small groups to actually practice doing it. Then each of us presented our unique grocery lists that we were given. They made us engage in the learning process and taught us what to do using PICTURES, not words. Despite feeling the need to take a memory course, I actually remember most of the details from that session all these years later! **The main take-a-way for me was that visualizations made me RETAIN details long term!**

❗ Using effective VISUALS that actually relate to the messaging and ENGAGING the audience through execution is the key to memorable presentations!

Wouldn't you like each of your clients or potential clients to remember what you taught them? The secret is in getting them to visualize and engage. This should sound familiar. This is why your participation in the exercises is so important!

Remember in Chapter 2, I suggested that a slide deck could be created without words? This chapter will help you take the results from your Diagnostics Discussion and create custom presentations using very few words but using many visualizations and stories.

Think about what you learned in *What Great Salespeople Do*. You want to be telling a story with every point you make. The better visualization you create for your audience, the more likely you will be able to increase your chances of them remembering and getting engaged.

❝❝ Telling a story AT them is not as powerful as INSPIRING THEM TO TELL THEIR OWN STORY!

As Dale Carnegie taught us almost one hundred years ago, nothing sounds sweeter than the sound of your own name. **Get the client to tell their story, and give that story back to them in a beautiful visualization and you WILL make an incredible impact.**

This chapter will help you transform their responses into a deliverable that will have meaning and allow you to explain why you will be able to help transform their weak and moderate performance into additional strengths.

The Three R's – RELATE – Make or Show a Connection Between Making Visuals Personal During Meetings

Almost every sales book emphasizes the importance of establishing rapport with your client. In fact, there are probably more books written about Relationship Selling than any other topic. If it were easy, there would be no need for this type of training or education. The words relate, relationship, and rapport are also interchangeable. Using a Neuroscience approach in the client/vendor communication process will help catapult relationships into a solid and credible status.

In the 90's I hosted a meeting in Colorado with executives from a Houston Oil Company. This was before Facebook and LinkedIn but we did have Google. So I searched for the attendees on their webpages; I searched for bios; and I searched for their names. It just so happened that the leader of the team popped up in my search because an article had been written about him and his miniature train collection that included an incredible photo of this man with his trains.

When the clients walked into the conference room to begin the meeting, this train photo of the senior level executive was projected on the screen with a "Welcome" message for the entire team. I also had a flip chart off to the side with every attendee's name hand written on the chart with space to the right of each name and a header above the blank space saying "Meeting Objective and Desired Outcome."

As each person walked into the conference room, the first thing they saw was a giant photo of their leader having fun with trains and a flip chart with each name written on it. You could feel the energy in the room as each attendee saw the photo as well as their own names. This is so unusual for a sales presentation to start with the focus on the attendees versus the host company and its product or service being offered. Why?

Most companies hosting clients will begin a presentation by projecting slides and photos of their own company. In contrast, by starting a meeting projecting client centric information, the client will know immediately that this meeting was about THEM. We did end up winning their business but more importantly the meeting kicked off with a fantastic icebreaker. Even the people working for him were unaware of this train hobby. We all learned a lot about the leader. He seemed more humanized and approachable and the rest of the meeting was very relaxed and even fun. By focusing on the client, what we also communicated was that our company culture was one in which they would want to do business. **A connection was estab-**

lished that made each person in that room RELATE to each other on an emotional level instantly.

This was a powerful and positive impact on the overall feeling during the meeting thanks to the power of visualization. That meeting is remembered ten years later by my coworkers and clients thanks to visualizations that were about them versus what we wanted to sell them.

If you don't like flip charts, you can also create a sign-in sheet to pass around asking for contact information. Be sure you also include an area on the form to list each person's primary objective for a successful meeting. This will help remind the facilitator of the meeting to ensure that the audience members feel special by addressing and documenting each of their priorities in the meeting.

The data collected and documented on the flip chart will also help you with a recap email thanking the attendees and keeping track of any action items that were flushed out during the meeting. I will not dive any deeper into post sales meeting response and tracking because that will be the focus of Part Three in this series. A Joint Execution Plan will be created from what is gathered during the first meeting and will include actions, dates, and accountability details. As you may recall reading, many sales people leave meetings feeling that they nailed it. They witnessed the client heads bobbing up and down in agreement yet when they called for the follow-up discussion, the client went dark. Per the books on Neuroscience that I mentioned, this would be because the salesperson did not articulate a strong value in the first meeting.

If you research your clients prior to the meeting and ask them what they want to accomplish, the "Fight or Flight" instinct will be defused. This will aid in collection of the data that will be converted and translated into a valuable deliverable that will ensure that critical second meeting.

Imagine starting a discussion with a visual like THIS one:

How well do you think your client would RELATE to this approach?

The Three R's – REPEAT – Do Something Again or a Number of Times

Most sales people don't consider that the audience they present to may not be the final decision makers. Even if you are selling to the CEO of a Corporation, often he or she must get approval by a Board of Trustees to protect stockholders and investors. Other organizations require a Steering Committee to make a decision and present to other stakeholders within an organization for final approvals. This means that your message must be REPEATABLE without your assistance.

Once you have translated the data from the Visnostic Statements and categorized each segment by strengths, challenges, and moderate areas, you will design a customized deliverable. **This document should be simple enough that your client can take it and REPEAT your message with the same quality that you articulated.** Having the appropriate visualization in this deliverable is important. Be careful because many charts can be just as much work translating as a document full of words and letters. KEEP IT SIMPLE so the client can't fail as he or she shares the report internally on your behalf.

I personally don't like a lot of Gantt charts or bar graphs for visuals because they require almost as much thinking as the binary numbers translated in Exercise #2. I prefer dashboards like the one pictured here. I would change the wording on this to soften the bad news around weak performance. From left to right, I would label these Challenges, Moderate, Strengths, and Outstanding. I avoid words like Bad, Lacking, Weakness, or Average. These can trigger emotions that we don't want our clients to experience.

❝❝ We want clients to know that we aren't judging or condemning them.
We are here to help any areas that aren't their strength to become a strength.

With companies like Tableau and qlik, visual scorecards are becoming much more interesting to look at than those old fashioned bar graphs typically generated using a spreadsheet. Tableau awards thirty experts, the title of Zen Master each year. A Zen Master is working with me to help DynaExec clients really maximize the impact of visualization in the deliverable. Here is an example of a visual that she created after reviewing the template that I had help developing. These can be customized during workshops or you can contract a consulting firm like Teknion Data Solutions to help create the right deliverable for you and your company.

You will convert the Diagnostic Statement responses into a document you will return to the client. You may want to change the name of the deliverable but I call it *The Insight Report*. This report will summarize and compliment the client's strong areas. In addition, it will identify areas that are more challenging and need improvement along with an explanation of how you can convert the non-strength areas into strengths.

❝❝ More importantly, this report will map your potential solutions to the client's weaker areas. This will allow you the opportunity to describe how you and your company will help those areas become strengths.

You may want to create additional value by including other comparative responses. Your clients will appreciate knowing how their performance compares to your existing clients, the competition, or perhaps other attendees during a conference. Other comparisons can be created based upon geography, segmentation, or an area specifically important in your industry.

Info graphics have become extremely desirable the past five years. Having a format similar to this is visually appealing and easy to understand. Here is an example of a Pizza company (first column) and how they compare to three of their competitors:

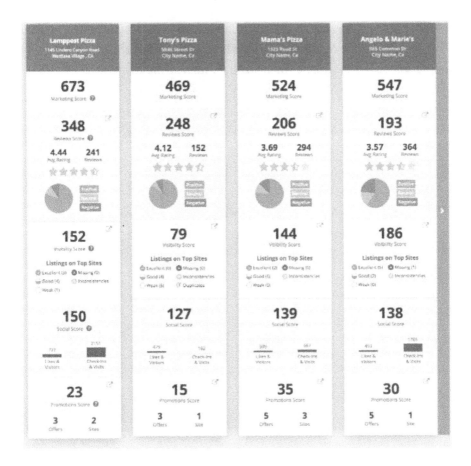

Creating simple visuals will help your client be effective as they RE-PEAT these results and recommendations internally.

Your Visualization Diagnostic Statements will be well received if they are accompanied by graphics that accomplish the **Three R's—Retain, Relate, & Repeat.**

DynaExec hosts Insight Workshops that will identify and develop a customized deliverable that your clients will value. This deliverable will practically ensure that you get that coveted second meeting and continue the sales process to closure.

Now that we have covered some ideas on visual aids, let's get into the most difficult content. Chapter Five will cover sample formulas to automate the diagnostics workbook that you have created.

CHAPTER FIVE

Creating a Valued Deliverable

Creating a Deliverable That Is Valued By The Client.

When you think of marketing tools, what comes to mind? Perhaps you imagine a presentation, brochure, website, an infographic, or a marketing video. I would agree that these are probably the most common marketing tools.

? **What if marketing gave sales a tool that helped translate features and functions into results that clients could visualize and understand?**

What if this tool then translated the clients' visualizations into an insightful deliverable with graphics? What if these graphics told a story of the clients' strengths? What if the client story included mapping your company's potential solutions to ensure all non-strengths become strengths?

This deliverable is in a different league; it is something completely outside the box of what marketing typically creates. Yet, it is something that clients will treasure and not want to discard or file away because they have helped create this amazing deliverable. It will be different from what all the other stereotypical sales people provide the client. The sales person will be viewed as a Client Business Strategist, not someone that will engage the fight or flight instinct.

If you don't already have at least ten powerful Diagnostics Statements written, you need to stop reading and go create them. After they are completed, be sure to identify a segment for each statement. These can include categories such as financial benefits, technology, consulting, additional services, training, legal, employee benefits, products, and any other offerings available from your company. I recommend you highlight each segment with a different color on your Diagnostic Statement worksheet to make it easier to see the different segments/categories. This will help you sort and organize the statements into a logical flow. Start with your most compelling statements in order to make the quickest impact on your client.

This is the most important chapter and it may be the most difficult for many readers because it is technical in nature. Don't let that scare you. I encourage you to work with IT coworkers to create formulas specific to your tool. I worked with my favorite coding expert, Ryan Wicks, to create a template that you might be able to leverage as a foundation for your own tool.

My goal is to eventually convert this spreadsheet into a software program or app. But for now, anybody can create a spreadsheet that will work. If you create a new tool, I would love for you to share your format!

Character	Binary Code	Character	Binary Code	Character	Binary Code	Character	Binary Code	Character	Binary Code
A	01000001	Q	01010001	g	01100111	w	01110111	-	00101101
B	01000010	R	01010010	h	01101000	x	01111000	.	00101110
C	01000011	S	01010011	i	01101001	y	01111001	/	00101111
D	01000100	T	01010100	j	01101010	z	01111010	0	00110000
E	01000101	U	01010101	k	01101011	!	00100001	1	00110001
F	01000110	V	01010110	l	01101100	"	00100010	2	00110010
G	01000111	W	01010111	m	01101101	#	00100011	3	00110011
H	01001000	X	01011000	n	01101110	$	00100100	4	00110100
I	01001001	Y	01011001	o	01101111	%	00100101	5	00110101
J	01001010	Z	01011010	p	01110000	&	00100110	6	00110110
K	01001011	a	01100001	q	01110001	'	00100111	7	00110111
L	01001100	b	01100010	r	01110010	(	00101000	8	00111000
M	01001101	c	01100011	s	01110011	)	00101001	9	00111001
N	01001110	d	01100100	t	01110100	*	00101010	?	00111111
O	01001111	e	01100101	u	01110101	+	00101011	@	01000000
P	01010000	f	01100110	v	01110110	,	00101100	_	01011111

For retention purposes, I have mentioned multiple times that our brains are a lot like a computer. Computers convert 1's and 0's to something on our computer screens that we can comprehend. Our brains do the same thing when they convert letters and words to physical things that we visualize. This is a major point because I have observed that salespeople make their clients' brains work way too hard. The easier we make the analysis process for our clients, the more likely they are to see the value we provide and award us their business instead of our competitors. Today, most salespeople give out the popular marketing tools and expect their clients to do the translating.

We also make our sales teams think too much. When done correctly, this tool can automatically map the potential solutions to the non-strength areas identified by the Visnostic Statements.

Once you have collected the responses your clients, giving them the Visnostic Statements with their responses means you would be basically handing them what they just told you. So you haven't told them anything they don't already know. Where is the value in that? If you do this, chances are, you won't be invited back for the next meeting.

There was a story in the Foreword from *The Challenger Sale* that described a client's attitude towards a sales rep that they really liked. However, the client admitted that they purchased from her competitor because they were perceived as adding more value. Translating what they told you into something revealing is great way to add value.

With this approach, you WILL win business even if you didn't have a strong relationship at the beginning of the sales cycle. In fact, the credibility earned during this process will catapult your relationship status to an excellent rating!

I hope you are starting to see how all the books I referenced in the preface compliment each other. I know I shared a story about giving a filled out form to my client and he was thrilled with that as my deliverable, but that is rare and cannot be expected in every sales scenario.

Let's discuss how you can create an incredible deliverable that your client will want to circulate internally. This deliverable is so powerful that it will transform your client into a coach, champion, and advocate. Why? They would love to create this for themselves, they will be grateful to you for taking that off his or her plate. YOU ARE DOING THE WORK FOR YOUR CLIENT!

So basically the Diagnostic Statement process accomplishes the following milestones:

1. It allows the client to tell you how to sell to them.

2. It provides clarity in how you prioritize your sales discussions. I have sold software my entire career and most software is so robust (ie complex) that you would put your client into a coma covering all the areas in which your software will enrich their lives. So the Diagnostic Statement exercise will uncover specific areas in which you can focus your sales efforts and spare the client from all the other alternatives you can provide (for now).

3. You identify each strength and weakness. However, you are not calling them out or insulting them because the negative information came from them, not you.

4. Even the areas in which they "CAN" do this today are scored. This scoring is one through five with one being that they do it today but it needs a lot of improvement and five being that things are perfect. So even a comment that says they can do it today can be just as much of a sales opportunity as a response of "I WISH we could do this today."

5. Your client becomes emotionally engaged. The statement methodology inspires them to envision scenes from his or her past or present. This engages emotions that surface resulting in comprehension of your message much more effectively than a slide presentation.

But all of these points are just DATA. It is up to "The Challenger Sales Professional" to convert that data into valuable information and paint the vision of how the clients' lives will be improved.

Creating the Translation Formulas -

1. Create a workbook with four worksheets.

   Label the main worksheet Diagnostics. This is where your statements and client responses will reside. This is the only part of the workbook that your client may see.

   It is also the only worksheet that will be altered. All other sheets are static and should remain locked to avoid accidental modifications to the formulas.

   As stated multiple times, do not give this to your client electronically. Allowing them to see the formulas could take away the allure of your final deliverable. Notice the different shadings for each segment. This makes it easier to identify by offering.

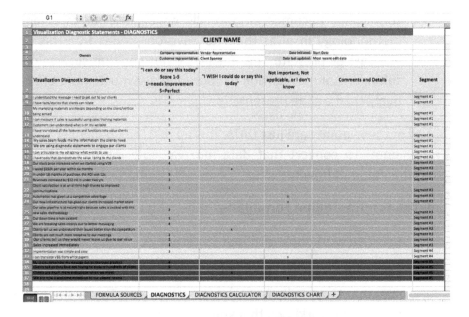

This template is extremely scalable. When adding lines to different segments, just be sure you label the segments correctly and the formulas will pick up the addition and make the appropriate adjustments.

2. Create a worksheet called Formula Sources. This will be a reference used for formulas. This is also the location for the details of the dashboard. This is static and requires no alterations or edits.

B20				*fx*	= SUM(B13:B16) – SUM(B11,B19)		

	A	B	C	D
1	0 - I WISH	0		
2	1 - Yes, but needs improvement	1		
3	2 - Yes, Below Average	2		
4	3 - Yes, Average	3		
5	4 - Yes, Above Average	4		
6	5 - Yes, Perfect	5		
7	N/A - Not Important, Unknown	N/A		
8				
9	Pointer Start Minimum	1		
10	Pointer Start Maximum	179		
11	Pointer Width (2 recommended)	1		
12				
13	Chart Series Green Width	60		
14	Chart Series Yellow Width	60		
15	Chart Series Red Width	60		
16	Chart Series Blank Width (Bottom)	180		
17				
18	Diagnostic Dynamic Chart Point Value	1.432		
19	Diagnostic Pointer Start Value	94.512		
20	Diagnostic Pointer End Value	264.488		
21				
22				
23				
24				
25				

FORMULA SOURCES / DIAGNOSTICS / DIAGNOSTICS CALCULATOR / DIAGNOSTICS CHART

3. Create a worksheet called Diagnostic Calculator. This area will calculate the totals for each of the Segments. For example, if a segment has two statements, the possible high score would be 5x2=10. But if you have a segment with 10 statements, the possible high score would be 5x10=50. So a 10 on the first example would create a dashboard in the green (strength) area, while a 10 on the second example would create a dashboard in the red (challenges/weaknesses) area.

This is also the area that has formulas stored. Once you have the first line of formulas, the other lines can be slightly modified to complete your worksheet. Here are some examples of formulas:

B2 = COUNTIF(DIAGNOSTICS! $F$8:$F$107, $A2)

C2 = ($B2 - $F2) * MAX('FORMULA SOURCES'! $B$1:$B$7)

D2 = SUMIFS(DIAGNOSTICS! $B$8:$B$107, DIAGNOSTICS! $F$8:$F$107, $A2, DIAGNOSTICS! $C$8:$C$107, "", DIAG-NOSTICS! $D$8:$D$107, "")

E2 = COUNTIFS(DIAGNOSTICS! $F$8:$F$107, $A2, DIAGNOS-TICS! $C$8:$C$107, ">""")

F2 = COUNTIFS(DIAGNOSTICS! $F$8:$F$107, $A2, DIAGNOS-TICS! $D$8:$D$107, ">""")

		C2	‡	fx	= ($B2 − $F2) * MAX('FORMULA SOURCES'!$B$1:$B$7)		
	A	B	Your Possible Score (Based on Applicable Challenges)	"I can do this today" Total Score	"I WISH" Items	"Not Applicable" Items	Industry Average	Our Average
1	Segment	Total Items						
2	Segment #1	8	35	19	0	1		
3	Segment #2	2	10	2	0	0		
4	Segment #3	14	60	26	2	2		
5	Segment #4	2	5	5	0	1		
6	Segment #5	4	15	10	1	1		
7								
8	All Segments	30	125	62	3	5	0	0
9								

This template has five different segments but this is not the limit. If you want to add more segments, you simply copy Row 6 and paste it in Row 7 and the formulas will modify automatically.

Columns G and H are not completed but are represented because it is intended to house data from collections to be averaged. Examples would be comparing individual responses to totals from an event or your client base. This will not be covered in this book but it is covered in the workshops.

4. Your fourth worksheet will be called Diagnostics Chart. This is where your graphs will be created automatically. You will save these charts for you final deliverable.

Diagnostic Results

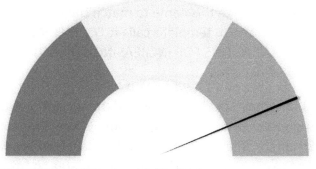

Diagnostic Results

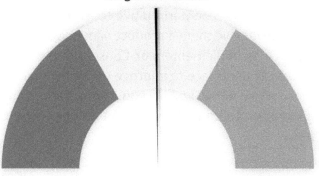

Diagnostic Results

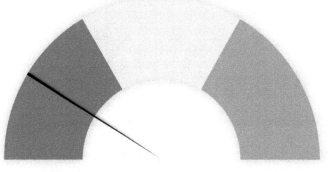

Once these four worksheets are setup, you will create a fifth worksheet that will be the deliverable. I like to call this a "Client Insight Report." You can change this name to match the objective of the deliverable. The workbook template calls it "CLIENT INSIGHT REPORT AND RECOMMENDATIONS FOR INCREASING STRENGTHS"

I designed this page so that when you fill out the Diagnostic sheet, it will populate these fields to avoid redundant entry. It looks a lot like the Diagnostics page. However, Column G has "Proposed Plan to Increase Strength." This is where you will explain how you will enable the prospective client to turn their challenged areas or moderate areas into strengths.

You may be tempted to simply put the name of the product or service in here but that is counterintuitive to everything you have just been taught! Never give them a product name. Work with your technical team such as Implementers or Consultants to summarize the PROCESS that will take place to improve the performance. If you put a product or service name, you have just gone back to your old ways of forcing the client to translate your terminology into what they can understand.

Most likely, you will need to reorganize these line items. Keep them in order by segment when filling out the statements but later, you will want to sort them based upon the scoring and level of strength identified.

Always start with the good news, which includes the strongest areas. This will be accomplished based upon the scores by segment. For example, if someone says "I can do this today" and they scored a 5 in each of five statements, their score would be 25 out of a potential 25. That would be a strength area.

However, if they responded "I WISH" in those five areas, it would be a challenge. The template has predefined scores. However, you may edit them if you determine different scores would be more appropriate for your business.

You will also have a midrange score that you also want to call out in your report as "Potential Improvements." With the two areas in which you identify weak or potential, you will then have the opportunity to give a summary of how your company can turn the weaknesses into strengths and the midrange responses into strengths as well.

If you conduct a workshop with DynaExec, I will provide a spreadsheet template to get you started. Or your IT department can help you fill out the form automatically based upon the Diagnostics your client fills out.

You will want to enhance this Insight document with charts and graphs and the best way to do that is to track all responses you receive and let your client know how they compare to others. For example, if you were at a show or conference, your goal would be to conduct as many of these diagnostics as possible. You can then collect all responses and let each one know how they compared to other attendees at that specific event or show.

You will have a fantastic reason to follow-up after the show with each person you interviewed. This should help you get that face-to-face meeting after your event. You would never want to just send the Insight report to your client without being there to walk him or her through it.

Another great way to approach this is to first contact at least ten existing clients and go through this process with them. Collect all those responses and use your client responses as your baseline. You can then approach potential clients and compare their answers with your client answers. In theory, the non-clients should score well below your existing clients, which will demonstrate true improvements to the potential client. This is actually my favorite approach because if you created the right Visnostic Statements, your clients should respond with 5's on all the "We CAN say this today" areas. This sends a strong message to your potential clients that your existing ones are confirming the accuracy of your statement results. In addition, this should make your prospective clients eager to join in on the success!

There is one final bonus for taking time to interview your client base with Visnostic Statements; if you have a segment offering that your client was unaware, you may find yourself with an extremely easy revenue growth opportunity!

Here is another example of an Insight Report Format. However, this is just a concept outline and to my knowledge, has never been used. I am sharing it because some people prefer to merge worksheets with documents. This demonstrates how flexible and customized the final deliverable can be. I look forward to receiving examples of creations from my readers.

VisNostic Selling

(YOUR COMPANY NAME) Insight
Results Diagnostic Statements

Company Participating in Research Call – _____ Contact - _____ Phone - _____ Email - _____

COMPANY SNAPSHOT	
Business Description - Overview • Collect any relevant details such as revenues • Collect any relevant details such as number of employees - • Collect any relevant details such as current provider- • Other	Scores from Diagnostic Statements – Summary by Segment - Scores • Employee Skills - • Technology - • Compliance - • Finance -

TOP STRENGTHS IDENTIFIED	BUSINESS IMPACT	HOW (YOUR COMPANY) CLIENTS ADDRESS

TOP CHALLENGES IDENTIFIED	BUSINESS IMPACT	HOW (YOUR COMPANY) CLIENTS ADDRESS

POTENTIAL IMPROVEMENTS IDENTIFIED	BUSINESS IMPACT	HOW (YOUR COMPANY) CLIENTS ADDRESS

YOUR COMPANY BEST PRACTICES	NOTES AND DESCRIPTIONS

There are two areas in which your client will see the most value. The first will be comparing how they do things today with another category. But the most impactful information that your client wants and needs will be your response how you can convert their non-strength areas into additional strengths.

Finally, here is a word of caution as you design your deliverable; do not attempt to use their own words to "customize" your potential solution! You may be tempted to coincidentally map your products or services exactly to their needs, but you risk losing credibility, trust, and the relationship. Do not insult their intelligence by repackaging what they told you as your deliverable.

Once again, I am looking forward to hearing from readers on creative modifications of these deliverables. Please send copies to me so I can recognize your efforts in future editions.

If all this still seems overwhelming, don't hesitate to reach out for assistance.

Other Ways To Add Value with Visnostic Statements!

I participated in a rather large meeting with a client that had been in merger and acquisition mode. The audience was full of people from all over the country. Almost all of them were from locations that had been acquired and were now teammates and yet they were all meeting each other for the first time – during my presentation! As we were planning for the meeting, we predicted that there might be some reluctance to share information with us because members of the audience may be uncomfortable with the newly formed organization.

Many people in your audience may be concerned about job security; therefore openly discussing their individual challenges didn't seem like the politically smart thing to share with a room full of strangers. So we leaned on the sponsor of the meeting. He shared with us important background on each team and several individuals. We went into that meeting knowing which people were the decision makers, what topics to avoid, what challenges had already been uncovered and we created a slide that was full of Visnostic Statements.

I know that this contradicts pretty much this entire book because the slide was full of bullets and letters. However, it ended up being the only slide we showed all day because the silence and reservation from the audience transformed into stimulating collaboration. The audience realized they each were experiencing many of the same challenges and had empathy for each other. This was an incredible scenario to witness. We were no longer sales people. We became facilitators of a valuable conversation and team building exercise. We became Business Strategists versus that horrible stereotype associated with Sales People. We even changed our titles after this meeting.

I wish there was a cookie cutter methodology that every single one of us could use on every single client. That would make things pretty easy. However, the beauty of sales is that each client and each sales process is like a fingerprint; while they all look very similar, they will each be unique. How you deliver your message will be dependent upon each unique client and diagnostics outcome. However, here are some tips that I believe will ensure your success:

1. While this approach is much more flexible than a presentation, it is important that you conduct the Visnostic Statements in person. Never hand the tool to the client and ask them to fill it out and return it to you. You will be missing out on the important body language, the collaboration, and the elaborate responses. You will learn more during the client's envision process than the responses themselves. In most conversations, I can't write fast enough because the client has so much they want to share.

2. Always reach out to the client **within twelve hours** of leaving your meeting with a summary of what you discussed and a timeline from which they can expect a deliverable. If you wait longer than that, you and the conversation will be a distant memory and you will have lost your momentum and the client's interest.

3. Always set a date and time for that second meeting to go over the results in person. Again, do not be tempted to email the Insight report to the client. You will miss out on important dialogue and body language. Be face-to-face for that meeting to ensure you have 100% of their attention and they aren't asleep or creating some sort of to-do list.

4. Print out and keep hard copies of the Visnostic Statements with you at all times. These conversations can happen at any location, any time, and do not need any technology to be conducted. Take advantage of that!

5. Also keep copies on your mobile devices. I like to send copies to my iPhone and then open and save it in my iBooks. You never know when that electronic copy will come in handy.

6. Work with marketing to design graphics that represent each Diagnostic Statement. Showing graphics as you go over the statements will make a huge emotional impact that will be remembered.

I predicted that Chapters Four and Five would be more difficult to read. For one thing, cartoon drawings were replaced with screen shots. In addition, the first three chapters were written with more emotional content and hopefully you felt your own enthusiasm brewing as you read. However, due to the nature of the technical content, the last chapters were extremely cerebral. Remember that people buy based upon emotion, not logic. This is because humans enjoy feeling various emotions. While some people do enjoy cerebral content, the majority of people prefer to be entertained and have their feelings engaged.

If for some reason you still don't feel prepared to go execute these new skills, I offer three different types of one-day workshops to ensure success:

1. **Creating Visnostic Statements**. This is typically done with marketing and sales. We evaluate existing content and translate it by segmentation.

2. **Creating the potential solutions that map to each Diagnostic Statement**. This is typically conducted with consultants, engineers, implementers, and technical support personnel.

3. **Sales Training.** In addition to the new tool, the content in this book should also inspire the creation of new pre-

sentations, brochures, infographics, videos, websites, and other corporate messaging. However, I see great things created all the time that fail because execution didn't happen at the field level. I will teach the concepts and stories of this book to the sales organization to ensure they are passionate and confident in the various ways these tools can be leveraged.

I look forward to working with as many of you as possible to ensure your success!

CONCLUSION

Congratulations for investing time to learn about Visualization Diagnostic Statements! I look forward to hearing from each of you about the ways in which it has touched your life and your clients' lives as well.

This book was written differently than most business books you have read in the past. I have been using specific tactics to help you retain the information you just read. Let's see if it worked; try and repeat what you read when you saw these graphics.

Did Fight or Flight pop into your head?

Do you remember the story that went with this next graphic?

What were the lessons learned during the exercise that leveraged this drawing?

Wouldn't you love it if your clients thought of the benefits you could bring to their organizations after seeing specific pictures? Wouldn't it be awesome if your clients could repeat your presentation internally? If so, you now know the secrets to making that happen!

The steps you just read are things that I have never documented and have only partially shared with various sales teams that reported to me. One reason I have guarded this approach is because I believe one reason these Diagnosis Statements are so powerful, is because nobody else does them. I am concerned that if this approach takes off, it will lose its magic.

So if you are one of the first to read this, I hope you have a sense of urgency to get out there and execute before millions of other sales people start doing the same thing and it loses what makes it unique.

I want to stress that this is not a hypothesis. This approach has made me exceed my sales numbers when not one other salesperson on the team was able to hit quota. It was my secret to being the number one sales person globally three years in a row with a very well known Japanese technology company. It feels good to share these secrets at this stage of my career and I am extremely excited to hear new stories of success from my readers. I fully expect to learn new and creative ways to execute this communication methodology from each of you.

I hope you were able to read this book in one sitting. My goal was to keep this book short and sweet because these concepts are new and can be difficult and time consuming to execute. But do not get discouraged if this feels uncomfortable. These feelings will subside because you WILL get better at this after you do it a few times.

I don't expect you to have passion for this approach after just reading a book. However, I DO expect that you will feel the same passion I have for this approach the first time you witness its power with your clients!

You have learned specific ways you can execute fundamentals from all three books mentioned in the Preface. My book focused on Why, How, and What needs to be done. Stories were in each chapter to help with memorization. In addition, graphics were a big part of this book to help with retention and to quickly reference specific areas. And finally, this is a very different sales approach and you have learned a unique way to challenge your clients to do things differently and better.

All three of these recommended books stated either blatantly or subliminally that the most successful sales people add value and do things differently than their competitors. The Diagnostic Statement approach is unusual and when done correctly will be welcomed by your client. This approach will defuse the Fight or Flight instinct. You will earn your clients respect because you will clearly paint a picture of how you will not only help them be better in several of their non-strength areas, but you just did most of the work for them in order to circulate your value internally. You will see your client become your biggest champion and coach because you just described how you could make them look good and catapult their career. You will now be a trusted advisor instead of a typical sales person trying to earn a commission check.

You should feel differently about yourself. Because of this new knowledge, I challenge you to reflect on your current title. If it is a sales title, account manager title, or anything that implies sales **I highly recommend that you consider changing your title immediately!** Even Mike Bosworth suggested changing titles in his Foreword. Do you recall what you learned about the Fight or Flight instinct within each of us? Why in the world would you have a title that discourages people from meeting with you? As you use this approach, you will become much more than a salesperson so your title should reflect that. I love the title, "Client Business Strategist." What client wouldn't want to meet with someone that has a title that is focused on THEM? And who doesn't appreciate someone that has a position that is intended to help clients with strategic execution?

Once you are confident with conversations leveraging Visnostic Statements, and especially when you start seeing the deliverables that you will be generating, you will no longer feel like a sales person anyway. Better yet, your clients won't view you as a sales person either.

Hold your head up high because you will become a true trusted advisor and once your clients start telling other clients about their experience with you, your career will soar. I am excited for each and every one of you but I am even more excited for your clients. They need this translation effort from you and they will appreciate you for doing the work for them.

Not only did you just read a book that can change the way you perform professionally, but with proper execution, it should also change your company and your clients' companies for the better! Please be sure and share your comments, suggestions, and stories! I look forward to reading every single email! I expect this book to go through multiple revisions based upon feedback I receive and stories shared with me, but I also look forward to providing the next two books very soon.

It was important that Part One of my series focused on sales success because this book will immediately increase sales revenues. Once I have the attention, credibility, and respect from sales leadership, then they will be more receptive to what I have to share about leadership practices that must change.

Now that you have read the entire book, how has your interpretation of this graphic changed since the warm up exercise in the Preface?

Lastly, as you read this explanation at the beginning of the book, it was probably a bit confusing. As you re-read it now, it should make more sense.

WHAT are Visualization Diagnostic Statements™?

NOTE - Also referred to as a VDS or Diagnostic Statement in this book.

A Visnostic or Visualization Diagnostic Statement is a trademarked term created by Kimberlee Slavik, CEO of DynaExec. It is a statement that requires a response from an audience. It stimulates emotional responses inspiring your audience to maximize their interest in your message.

The statements typically **translate** features and functions into something more meaningful to the audience.

A Diagnostic Statement often originates as an ineffective, generic, one-way **self-focused** message that has been converted into a meaningful two-way engaging statement that is **audience-focused**. Existing presentations, brochures, case studies, and other marketing materials are often reworded to become Visnostic Statements.

A Diagnostic Statement is also a qualification tool that will help you assess your audience. As you go through the statements, if your participant isn't responding or is struggling with responding, chances are high that you aren't in front of the right participant.

A Diagnostic Statement is also an effective way to determine if sales and marketing currently have the right messaging. If creating these statements feels effortless, the current messaging is strong. When these statements are difficult to create, the content doesn't contain what the clients need and want to know.

What's coming in Part Two –

This book is "Part One" of a series I have planned. If you feel a void, have a challenge in your career, or have a story worth sharing, please send your submissions to DynaExec@DynaExec.com. I sincerely want to address every request. My goal for future editions is to include stories from my readers.

Part One was very focused on a specific and powerful sales execution methodology. Part Two will focus on areas in which Sales Leadership must focus to create a culture and environment in which sales will thrive and prosper.

The topics that will be addressed in Part Two will be directed towards owners and senior leaders because during my career I have been part of way too many dysfunctional sales organizations. This dysfunction starts at the very top. If the owners or C-Level executive view sales with respect, others within the company will as well. However, most companies view sales as a necessary evil and this attitude ripples throughout the entire organization. In general, there just isn't much respect for sales professionals. Visions of the Used Car Salesman are a strong stereotype in many companies and as Part One explained, the Fight or Flight Syndrome is alive and well. You may think you appreciate your sales organization but you may be surprised to find out that your culture is not as healthy as you would like to believe. If you are one of the cultures that do not respect sales, you will observe a frustrated sales team, high turnover, and bad attitudes. Part Two will dissect the following topics:

Psychology and Salespeople –

There are two types of sales cultures in companies; One will fail and one will succeed.

1. Culture #1 - Sales is a necessary evil (no respect)

2. Culture #2 - Sales is the reason all jobs exist (respect)

Sales people get rejected almost every single day. Part Two will explain the importance of company support and offer specific ways a company must celebrate sales efforts. It will discuss the importance of paying your sales team WELL! The carrot must be attainable and the company must celebrate successes companywide. Leadership must also acknowledge, learn, and educate other departments on each failure to avoid repeating them.

Not everybody can sell. Don't try and convince yourself otherwise. Recognition is important. I have my own unique approach because "You are who you are, because of when you were, when." Because of my background, sales rejection doesn't bother me. I do sales for the affirmation. I do sales because I love my clients and I only want to work for companies that have outstanding offerings that make me passionate about what we have to sell. When I hire sales people, I look for people with thick skin. I look for people that are ok with rejection. However, I have yet to meet any thick skinned human being (I include myself in this statement) that can handle when the company they represent doesn't have his or her back. If the company is constantly trying to justify not paying, constantly playing down the significance of the efforts being made, belittling or disrespecting sales as an organization, there will be negative consequences.

The best companies pay very well and celebrate and reward sales with trips and awards and recognition. If the executives praise sales, the company will respect sales.

But if the executives do not respect sales, it WILL cost the company in morale, turnover, poor client relationships, lost credibility in the marketplace, and lost revenues. I see this most frequently in privately held companies. This is probably because commissions are literally coming out of the owners' pockets.

There is a way to turn this attitude around. And it's critical to do so because the commissions paid are much less than lost revenue due to high turnover or morale issues. Trust and support your sales and you WILL succeed with the right product/service, onboarding, support, and compensation plan! Many leaders will say they support sales but actions speak volumes and salespeople are highly fragile employees that can feel the slightest hint of doubt in a culture.

Part Two will cover why a strong work ethic, intelligence, analytical ability, integrity, and a fire in the belly are musts in hiring sales. If sales people don't want to work over 40 hours/week, something is either wrong with the culture or the employee. Figuring it out is critical and I will show you how to fix it.

Part Three will cover an area that is often ignored...the POST sales efforts. Many companies and cultures are structured where one part of the sales force invests time in building relationships only to have those relationships given to a new person to grow. Part Three will prove why this is bad for the client, the salesperson, the new salesperson, and the entire company. Part three will also focus on building an impeccable image with clients by managing a sales cycle as a Project Manager would manage a project.

These additional books will take what was taught in Part One to a completely different level! Your brand new Visualization Diagnostic Statement workbook tool will double in size and become a valued communication tool by your clients. I hope you are as excited to read the content in these books, as I am to share them!

Thank you! Happy Selling!

APPENDIX
Sales Basics Review, Tips, and Answers

neu·ro·sci·ence

ˈn(y)o͞orōˌsīəns/

noun

noun: **neuroscience**; plural noun: **neurosciences**

Any or all of the sciences, such as neurochemistry and experimental psychology, which deal with the structure or function of the nervous system and brain.

Body Language Basics –

- Looking to Their Right = Auditory Thought (Remembering a song)

- Looking to Their Left = Visual Thought (Remembering the color of a dress)

- Looking Down to Their Right = Someone creating a feeling or sensory memory (Thinking what it would be like to swim in jello)

- Looking Down to Their Left = Someone talking to themselves

Binary Conversion Chart –

Character	Binary Code	Character	Binary Code	Character	Binary Code	Character	Binary Code	Character	Binary Code
A	01000001	Q	01010001	g	01100111	w	01110111	-	00101101
B	01000010	R	01010010	h	01101000	x	01111000	.	00101110
C	01000011	S	01010011	i	01101001	y	01111001	/	00101111
D	01000100	T	01010100	j	01101010	z	01111010	0	00110000
E	01000101	U	01010101	k	01101011	!	00100001	1	00110001
F	01000110	V	01010110	l	01101100	"	00100010	2	00110010
G	01000111	W	01010111	m	01101101	#	00100011	3	00110011
H	01001000	X	01011000	n	01101110	$	00100100	4	00110100
I	01001001	Y	01011001	o	01101111	%	00100101	5	00110101
J	01001010	Z	01011010	p	01110000	&	00100110	6	00110110
K	01001011	a	01100001	q	01110001	'	00100111	7	00110111
L	01001100	b	01100010	r	01110010	(	00101000	8	00111000
M	01001101	c	01100011	s	01110011	)	00101001	9	00111001
N	01001110	d	01100100	t	01110100	*	00101010	?	00111111
O	01001111	e	01100101	u	01110101	+	00101011	@	01000000
P	01010000	f	01100110	v	01110110	,	00101100	_	01011111

Basic Sales Psychology Principles -

Sales rejection is partially due to human natures resistance to being persuaded. Winning a point or argument is what humans want and need.

Good Pain and Bad Pain -

People buy due to pain (GOOD pain is caused by things like rapid growth, lack of resources, supply chain issues, etc. and BAD pain is caused by things like no growth, layoffs necessary, too much stock, etc.) A good salesperson will be attempting to uncover pain throughout the sales process.

Terminology –

B2B – Business to Business – When a company sells to another company.

Example: A computer manufacturer will sell wholesale to a retail store versus the consumer.

B2C – Business to Consumer – When a company sells to the end user.

Example: When a retail store sells directly to the consumer.

Some companies have distribution models that are both B2B and B2C.

The Art of Answering Questions -

Never ask closed ended questions – Yes and No answers can be blurted out without any thought behind the answer. Open-ended questions have problems as well because they can go in many different directions and you lose focus on the original intent. Having multiple-choice is the best way for the audience to ponder and consider the options. They have to think harder to answer, which is how you get people emotionally engaged.

Studies have shown that giving people options, triggers chemicals in the brain to choose one. For example – if you say "Will you buy from me?" Yes or No? It is way too easy to say No. If you give your client three pricing/package options from which to choose, they will typically chose one. So it is an automatic YES. So when I am responded to an RFP (Request for Proposal), RFI (Request for Information, or a RFQ (Request for Quotation), I always provide three alternative pricing scenarios. The theory is that they choose one-option vs eliminating you from the other bids.

Very Important Point - When a client asks a question, you will automatically want to answer it. Instead, ask what is driving that specific question. Often, the real question is not what the client actually asked. When I go on sales calls with a Software Engineer, Technical Support, Management, or other teammates, their purpose for being on the call is usually to answer all questions sales can't handle. However, when questions arise, it is imperative to uncover what is driving the question so you don't get drug down the wrong path and derail the momentum of the meeting.

For example, I was in a meeting about three weeks before Thanksgiving and the client asked what was the average implementation time. This is a logical question and my engineer wanted to tell the client that the answer was six weeks. Instead of answering the question, I asked the client why this question was important and they responded with they wanted to make sure it could be completed before the holidays (which I just said was in three weeks). If we had answered the question with the "six weeks" response, the client would have jumped to the conclusion that we were not the appropriate solution and we would have lost the sale.

The real question the client wanted to ask was, "Could you have this implemented by the holidays?" And our answer would have been, "Yes, we will double up on resources to ensure implementation is complete by the holidays."

Potential Answers to EXERCISE #4 –

- ➢ I saved $150k per year within six months of purchasing a new software.

- ➢ In under 18 months of purchase, the ROI was 12x what I paid for my software.

- ➢ Revenues increased by $12 million in under two years due to increased client demand.

- ➢ Client satisfaction is at an all time high thanks to automation.

- ➢ Automation has given us a competitive advantage in the marketplace within six months but more importantly; our new service is giving our clients a competitive advantage as well.

- ➢ I am able to say we had an implementation that caused zero down time.

- ➢ I was promoted due to all these exciting improvements in our business.

BIOGRAPHIES

Author Bio and Resumé

Kimberlee Slavik - www.linkedin.com/in/kimslavik

Kimberlee is an award winning business strategist in the Information Technology (IT) industry, known for helping clients increase sales and profits by leveraging software, services, hardware, storage, business continuity, & cloud computing.

* @85 recommendations on LinkedIn from clients, peers, direct reports, indirect reports, and management validating accomplishments

* Sold or participated in selling over $1.9 billion worth of software, products, & services during a 20 year career

* Managed a complex, 70+ person storage team with P&L accountability for HP exceeding $900 million goal

* Numerous awards received for focusing on post-sales support and customer references

* Exceeded quota for 20 years averaging almost 200% of plan

* Start-up Expert – including SaaS, cloud, virtualization, storage, & BC

Specialties:

* Surpassing sales objectives

* Business acumen & P&L

* 15 yrs of people leadership

* Excellent communication & presentation skills

* Collaborative team player leading multiple teams towards a common goal

* Project management & organizational skills

* Organizational design & coaching high performance teams

* Enterprise channel strategy development & execution

* C-level executives & senior execs sales closures

* Indirect enterprise channel sales & marketing

* Cloud, software, BC, & Storage Sales

Summa Cum Laude from LaTourneau University, with a Bachelor of Science degree in Business Administration.

Certified by Southern Methodist University in "Leading the High-Performance Sales Organization."

Currently pursuing an MBA degree in International Business at Heriot-Watt Business School in Edinburgh, Scotland.

Foreword Bio and Resumé

Mike Bosworth - https://www.linkedin.com/in/mikebosworth/

Mike Bosworth has been a thought leader within the field of sales and marketing over the last several decades. He is an author, speaker, entrepreneur, story seeker and sales philosopher. Bosworth is the best-selling author of Solution Selling: Creating Buyers in Difficult Selling Markets (McGraw-Hill, 1993) co-author of Customer Centric Selling (McGraw-Hill, 2003) and co-author of What Great Salespeople Do: The Science of Selling Through Emotional Connection and The Power of Story (McGraw-Hill, 2012).

Mike Bosworth began his career in the information technology industry in 1972 on the Help Desk for Xerox Computer Services. He was their top new business salesperson in 1975, managed the "Branch of the Year" in 1979 and was promoted to Manager of Field Sales in 1980.

From 1976 through 1982 he designed and delivered sales training programs for Xerox's Computer Services Division. His years of field experience plus the knowledge he gained from working with Neil Rackham on the Xerox SPIN selling pilot project inspired him to found Solution Selling in 1983 with a mission to lift the bottom 80%. Solution Selling became one of the most widely adopted "customer usage training" methodologies in the technology industry.

In 2008, Mike realized that there was still a 'missing link' in understanding why such a small percentage of sellers generate such a large percentage of revenue. Mike's interest and research into how the very best sales professionals have high EQ and intuitively connect and build trust with buyers. This led him to build a framework around how to help the "bottom 80% boost their EQ with a connection framework based on the power of story." Mike founded Mike Bosworth Leadership in January 2013 to begin teaching salespeople and leaders to boost their EQ by using the power of storytelling and story tending to gain trust, and to influence without having to resort to using authority.

Bosworth has a degree in Business Management and Marketing from California State Polytechnic University.

In addition to his keynote speaking for professional associations and major corporations, he has been a featured lecturer at the Stanford Graduate School of Business, The Stanford Program on Market Strategy for Technology-Based Companies, The American Marketing Association Customer Message Management Forums, The Anderson School of Management At UCLA, the Paul Merage School of Business at UC Irvine, The University of Connecticut and Rollins College to name a few.

He lives with his wife Jennifer Lehr on Orcas Island, Washington.

Artist Bio and Resumé

David A. Wiener - https://www.linkedin.com/in/david-a-wiener-573b1a1/

David is an action-oriented generalist with diverse sales and marketing experience in high technology environments. After engineering design and system installation of cryogenic systems, he entered the selling world of investment brokerage of large apartment buildings.

Then, after a decade of real estate investment, he moved to the high tech industry. He has a strong focus on business start-up, market expansion, and turnaround situations. He demonstrated success in sales and sales management of system and application software as well as hardware. He has been successful at small and large companies and divisions of large companies starting new ventures. He has held positions up to and including VP Sales. He has held a TS clearance and has expertise with systems integrators and government programs.

After his career in high tech, David moved on to small farm communities in Florida, Texas and then upstate New York where he built a studio and produces his art of fine ink drawings, oil paintings and ceramics. He also spends his time working for his town as chair of the planning board. He also is a member of the County planning board and a board member of the town fire department.

Education: Newark College of Engineering - BSME, MSIE, MSCIS (abt)

For more information about David's artwork or to commission his talent, please visit http://artbydavidwiener.blogspot.com

CPSIA information can be obtained
at www.ICGtesting.com
Printed in the USA
FSHW020807030219
55449FS